CW00926123

Just The

factsl0l
Textbook Key Facts

Textbook Outlines, Highlights, and Practice Quizzes

Biopsychology

by John P.J. Pinel, 6th Edition

All "Just the Facts101" Material Written or Prepared by Cram101 Publishing

Title Page

STUDYING MADE EASY

This Cram101 notebook is designed to make studying easier and increase your comprehension of the textbook material. Instead of starting with a blank notebook and trying to write down everything discussed in class lectures, you can use this Cram101 textbook notebook and annotate your notes along with the lecture.

Our goal is to give you the best tools for success.

For a supreme understanding of the course, pair your notebook with our online tools. Should you decide you prefer Cram101.com as your study tool,

we'd like to offer you a trade...

Our Trade In program is a simple way for us to keep our promise and provide you the best studying tools, regardless of where you purchased your Cram101 textbook notebook. As long as your notebook is in *Like New Condition**, you can send it back to us and we will immediately give you a Cram101.com account free for 120 days!

Let The *Trade In* Begin!

THREE SIMPLE STEPS TO TRADE:

1. Go to www.cram101.com/tradein and fill out the packing slip information.

2. Submit and print the packing slip and mail it in with your Cram101 textbook notebook.

3. Activate your account after you receive your email confirmation.

* Books must be returned in *Like New Condition*, meaning there is no damage to the book including, but not limited to; ripped or torn pages, markings or writing on pages, or folded / creased pages. Upon receiving the book, Cram101 will inspect it and reserves the right to terminate your free Cram101.com account and return your textbook notebook at the owners expense.

Visit Cram101.com for full Practice Exams

"Just the Facts101" is a Cram101 publication and tool designed to give you all the facts from your textbooks. Visit Cram101.com for the full practice test for each of your chapters for virtually any of your textbooks.

Cram101 has built custom study tools specific to your textbook. We provide all of the factual testable information and unlike traditional study guides, we will never send you back to your textbook for more information.

YOU WILL NEVER HAVE TO HIGHLIGHT A BOOK AGAIN!

Cram101 StudyGuides

All of the information in this StudyGuide is written specifically for your textbook. We include the key terms, places, people, and concepts... the information you can expect on your next exam!

Want to take a practice test?

Throughout each chapter of this StudyGuide you will find links to cram101.com where you can select specific chapters to take a complete test on, or you can subscribe and get practice tests for up to 12 of your textbooks, along with other exclusive cram101.com tools like problem solving labs and reference libraries.

Cram101.com

Only cram101.com gives you the outlines, highlights, and PRACTICE TESTS specific to your textbook. Cram101.com is an online application where you'll discover study tools designed to make the most of your limited study time.

By purchasing this book, you get 50% off the normal monthly subscription fee!. Just enter the promotional code **'DK73DW9241'** on the Cram101.com registration screen.

www.Cram101.com

Learning System

facts101

Biopsychology
John P.J. Pinel, 6th

CONTENTS

Digit Span

Alcoholism

Korsakoff's syndrome

Neuron

Brain damage

Neuroimaging

Cognitive neuroscience

Critical thinking

Behavioral neuroscience

Neuroanatomy

Neurochemistry

Neuroendocrinology

Neuropathology

Neuropharmacology

Neurophysiology

Natural selection

Coolidge effect

Applied research

Case study

Chapter 1. Biopsychology as a Neuroscience What Is Biopsychology, Anyway?

CHAPTER OUTLINE: KEY TERMS, PEOPLE, PLACES, CONCEPTS

- Corpus callosum
- Curare
- Hypothalamus
- Physiological psychology
- Autonomic nervous system
- Cerebral cortex
- Neuropsychology
- Psychopharmacology
- Psychophysiology
- Neuropsychological assessment
- Cognition
- Comparative psychology
- Evolutionary psychology
- Thiamine
- Empirical method
- Motion perception
- Basal ganglia
- Caudate nucleus
- Morgan's Canon

Chapter 1. Biopsychology as a Neuroscience What Is Biopsychology, Anyway?

7

	Scientific journal
	Leucotome
	Lobotomy

Digit Span	In psychology and neuroscience, memory span is the longest list of items that a person can repeat back in correct order immediately after presentation on 50% of all trials. Items may include words, numbers, or letters. The task is known as digit span when numbers are used.
Alcoholism	Alcoholism is a broad term for problems with alcohol, and is generally used to mean compulsive and uncontrolled consumption of alcoholic beverages, usually to the detriment of the drinker's health, personal relationships, and social standing. It is medically considered a disease, specifically a neurological disorder, and in medicine several other terms are used, specifically 'alcohol abuse' and 'alcohol dependence,' which have more specific definitions. In 1979 an expert World Health Organization committee discouraged the use of 'alcoholism' in medicine, preferring the category of 'alcohol dependence syndrome'.
Korsakoff's syndrome	Korsakoff's syndrome is a neurological disorder caused by the lack of thiamine (vitamin B_1) in the brain. Its onset is linked to chronic alcohol abuse and/or severe malnutrition. The syndrome is named after Sergei Korsakoff, the neuropsychiatrist who popularized the theory.
Neuron	A neuron is an electrically excitable cell that processes and transmits information through electrical and chemical signals. A chemical signal occurs via a synapse, a specialized connection with other cells. Neurons connect to each other to form neural networks.
Brain damage	Brain damage is the destruction or degeneration of brain cells. Brain injuries occur due to a wide range of internal and external factors. A common category with the greatest number of injuries is traumatic brain injury (TBI) following physical trauma or head injury from an outside source, and the term acquired brain injury (ABI) is used in appropriate circles, to differentiate brain injuries occurring after birth, from injury due to a disorder or congenital malady.

Chapter 1. Biopsychology as a Neuroscience What Is Biopsychology, Anyway?

Neuroimaging	Neuroimaging includes the use of various techniques to either directly or indirectly image the structure, function/pharmacology of the brain. It is a relatively new discipline within medicine and neuroscience/psychology. Neuroimaging falls into two broad categories:•Structural imaging, which deals with the structure of the brain and the diagnosis of gross (large scale) intracranial disease (such as tumor), and injury, and•functional imaging, which is used to diagnose metabolic diseases and lesions on a finer scale (such as Alzheimer's disease) and also for neurological and cognitive psychology research and building brain-computer interfaces.
Cognitive neuroscience	Cognitive neuroscience is an academic field concerned with the scientific study of biological substrates underlying cognition, with a specific focus on the neural substrates of mental processes. It addresses the questions of how psychological/cognitive functions are produced by the brain. Cognitive neuroscience is a branch of both psychology and neuroscience, overlapping with disciplines such as physiological psychology, cognitive psychology and neuropsychology.
Critical thinking	Critical thinking is a type of reasonable, reflective thinking that is aimed at deciding what to believe or what to do. It is a way of deciding whether a claim is always true, sometimes true, partly true, or false. Critical thinking can be traced in Western thought to the Socratic method of Ancient Greece and in the East, to the Buddhist kalama sutta and Abhidharma.
Behavioral neuroscience	Behavioral neuroscience, biopsychology, or psychobiology is the application of the principles of biology (in particular neurobiology), to the study of physiological, genetic, and developmental mechanisms of behavior in human and non-human animals. It typically investigates at the level of nerves, neurotransmitters, brain circuitry and the basic biological processes that underlie normal and abnormal behavior. Most typically, experiments in behavioral neuroscience involve non-human animal models (such as rats and mice, and non-human primates) which have implications for better understanding of human pathology and therefore contribute to evidence-based practice.
Neuroanatomy	Neuroanatomy is the study of the anatomy and stereotyped organization of nervous systems. In contrast to animals with radial symmetry, whose nervous system consists of a distributed network of cells, animals with bilateral symmetry have segregated, defined nervous systems, and thus we can make much more precise statements about their neuroanatomy. In vertebrates, the nervous system is segregated into the internal structure of the brain and spinal cord (together called the central nervous system, or CNS) and the routes of the nerves that connect to the rest of the body (known as the peripheral nervous system, or PNS).
Neurochemistry	Neurochemistry is the specific study of neurochemicals, which include neurotransmitters and other molecules such as neuro-active drugs that influence neuron function.

Chapter 1. Biopsychology as a Neuroscience What Is Biopsychology, Anyway?

9

CHAPTER HIGHLIGHTS & NOTES: KEY TERMS, PEOPLE, PLACES, CONCEPTS

	This principle closely examines the manner in which these neurochemicals influence the network of neural operation. This evolving area of neuroscience offers a neurochemist a micro-macro connection between the analysis of organic compounds active in the nervous system and neural processes such as cortical plasticity, neurogenesis and neural differentiation.
Neuroendocrinology	Neuroendocrinology is the study of the extensive interactions between the nervous system and the endocrine system, including the biological features of the cells that participate, and how they functionally communicate. The nervous and endocrine systems often act together to regulate the physiological processes of the human body. Neuroendocrinology arose from the recognition that the brain, especially the hypothalamus, controls secretion of pituitary gland hormones, and has subsequently expanded to investigate numerous interconnections of the endocrine and nervous systems.
Neuropathology	Neuropathology is the study of disease of nervous system tissue, usually in the form of either small surgical biopsies or whole autopsy brains. Neuropathology is a subspecialty of anatomic pathology, neurology, and neurosurgery. It should not be confused with neuropathy, which refers to disorders of the nerves (usually in the peripheral nervous system).
Neuropharmacology	Neuropharmacology is a peer-reviewed scientific journal in the field of neuroscience. It was established in 1962 as the International Journal of Neuropharmacology and obtained its current name in 1970.
Neurophysiology	Neurophysiology is a part of physiology. Neurophysiology is the study of nervous system function. Primarily, it is connected with neurobiology, psychology, neurology, clinical neurophysiology, electrophysiology, biophysical neurophysiology, ethology, neuroanatomy, cognitive science and other brain sciences.
Natural selection	Natural selection is the process by which traits become more or less common in a population due to consistent effects upon the survival or reproduction of their bearers. It is a key mechanism of evolution. The natural genetic variation within a population of organisms may cause some individuals to survive and reproduce more successfully than others in their current environment.
Coolidge effect	In biology and psychology, the Coolidge effect is a phenomenon--seen in nearly every mammalian species in which it has been tested--whereby both males and females exhibit continuous high sexual performance given the introduction of new receptive partners.
Applied research	Applied research is a form of systematic inquiry involving the practical application of science. It accesses and uses some part of the research communities' (the academy's) accumulated theories, knowledge, methods, and techniques, for a specific, often state-, business-, or client-driven purpose.

Chapter 1. Biopsychology as a Neuroscience What Is Biopsychology, Anyway?

Case study	A case study is a research method common in social science. It is based on an in-depth investigation of a single individual, group, or event. Case studies may be descriptive or explanatory.
Corpus callosum	The corpus callosum, is a wide, flat bundle of neural fibers beneath the cortex in the eutherian brain at the longitudinal fissure. It connects the left and right cerebral hemispheres and facilitates interhemispheric communication. It is the largest white matter structure in the brain, consisting of 200-250 million contralateral axonal projections.
Curare	Curare /kju?'r??ri?/ is a common name for various arrow poisons originating from South America. The three main types of curare are:•tubocurare. It is a mono-quaternary alkaloid, an isoquinoline derivative.•calebas curare•pot curare. Of these three types, some formulas belonging to the calebas curare are the most toxic, relative to their LD values. History Curare was used as a paralyzing poison by South American indigenous people.
Hypothalamus	The Hypothalamus is a portion of the brain that contains a number of small nuclei with a variety of functions. One of the most important functions of the hypothalamus is to link the nervous system to the endocrine system via the pituitary gland (hypophysis). The hypothalamus is located below the thalamus, just above the brain stem.
Physiological psychology	Physiological psychology is a subdivision of behavioral neuroscience (biological psychology) that studies the neural mechanisms of perception and behavior through direct manipulation of the brains of nonhuman animal subjects in controlled experiments. Unlike other subdivisions within biological psychology, the main focus of physiological psychological research is the development of theories that describe brain-behavior relationships rather than the development of research that has translational value. It is sometimes alternatively called psychophysiology, and in recent years also cognitive neuroscience.
Autonomic nervous system	The autonomic nervous system is the part of the peripheral nervous system that acts as a control system functioning largely below the level of consciousness, and controls visceral functions. The Autonomic nervous system affects heart rate, digestion, respiration rate, salivation, perspiration, diameter of the pupils, micturition (urination), and sexual arousal. Whereas most of its actions are involuntary, some, such as breathing, work in tandem with the conscious mind.
Cerebral cortex	The cerebral cortex is a sheet of neural tissue that is outermost to the cerebrum of the mammalian brain.

Chapter 1. Biopsychology as a Neuroscience What Is Biopsychology, Anyway?

11

CHAPTER HIGHLIGHTS & NOTES: KEY TERMS, PEOPLE, PLACES, CONCEPTS

	It plays a key role in memory, attention, perceptual awareness, thought, language, and consciousness. It is constituted of up to six horizontal layers, each of which has a different composition in terms of neurons and connectivity.
Neuropsychology	Neuropsychology studies the structure and function of the brain as they relate to specific psychological processes and behaviors. It is seen as a clinical and experimental field of psychology that aims to study, assess, understand and treat behaviors directly related to brain functioning. The term neuropsychology has been applied to lesion studies in humans and animals.
Psychopharmacology	Psychopharmacology is the study of drug-induced changes in mood, sensation, thinking, and behavior. The field of psychopharmacology studies a wide range of substances with various types of psychoactive properties. The professional and commercial fields of pharmacology and psychopharmacology do not mainly focus on psychedelic or recreational drugs, as the majority of studies are conducted for the development, study, and use of drugs for the modification of behavior and the alleviation of symptoms, particularly in the treatment of mental disorders (psychiatric medication).
Psychophysiology	Psychophysiology is the branch of psychology that is concerned with the physiological bases of psychological processes. While psychophysiology was a general broad field of research in the 1960s and 1970s, it has now become quite specialized, and has branched into subspecializations. For example, Social Psychophysiology, Cardiovascular Psychophysiology, Cognitive Psychophysiology, and Cognitive Neuroscience.
Neuropsychological assessment	Neuropsychological assessment was traditionally carried out to assess the extent of impairment to a particular skill and to attempt to determine the area of the brain which may have been damaged following brain injury or neurological illness. With the advent of neuroimaging techniques, location of space-occupying lesions can now be more accurately determined through this method, so the focus has now moved on to the assessment of cognition and behaviour, including examining the effects of any brain injury or neuropathological process that a person may have experienced. A core part of neuropsychological assessment is the administration of neuropsychological tests for the formal assessment of cognitive function.
Cognition	In science, cognition is a group of mental processes that includes attention, memory, producing and understanding language, solving problems, and making decisions. Cognition is studied in various disciplines such as psychology, philosophy, linguistics, science and computer science.

Chapter 1. Biopsychology as a Neuroscience What Is Biopsychology, Anyway?

Comparative psychology	Comparative psychology refers to the scientific study of the behavior and mental processes of non-human animals, especially as these relate to the phylogenetic history, adaptive significance, and development of behavior. Research in this area addresses many different issues, uses many different methods, and explores the behavior of many different species, from insects to primates. Comparative psychology is sometimes assumed to emphasize cross-species comparisons, including those between humans and animals.
Evolutionary psychology	Evolutionary psychology is an approach in the social and natural sciences that examines psychological traits such as memory, perception, and language from a modern evolutionary perspective. It seeks to identify which human psychological traits are evolved adaptations - that is, the functional products of natural selection or sexual selection. Adaptationist thinking about physiological mechanisms, such as the heart, lungs, and immune system, is common in evolutionary biology.
Thiamine	Thiamine is a water-soluble vitamin of the B complex. First named aneurin for the detrimental neurological effects of its lack in the diet, it was eventually assigned the generic descriptor name vitamin B_1. Its phosphate derivatives are involved in many cellular processes. The best-characterized form is thiamine pyrophosphate (TPP), a coenzyme in the catabolism of sugars and amino acids. In yeast, TPP is also required in the first step of alcoholic fermentation.
Empirical method	The empirical method is generally taken to mean the approach of using a collection of data to base a theory or derive a conclusion in science. It is part of the scientific method, but is often mistakenly assumed to be synonymous with the experimental method. The empirical method is not sharply defined and is often contrasted with the precision of the experimental method, where data are derived from the systematic manipulation of variables in an experiment.
Motion perception	Motion perception is the process of inferring the speed and direction of elements in a scene based on visual, vestibular and proprioceptive inputs. Although this process appears straightforward to most observers, it has proven to be a difficult problem from a computational perspective, and extraordinarily difficult to explain in terms of neural processing. Motion perception is studied by many disciplines, including psychology (i.e. visual perception), neurology, neurophysiology, engineering, and computer science.
Basal ganglia	The basal ganglia are a group of nuclei of varied origin in the brains of vertebrates that act as a cohesive functional unit. They are situated at the base of the forebrain and are strongly connected with the cerebral cortex, thalamus and other brain areas.

Chapter 1. Biopsychology as a Neuroscience What Is Biopsychology, Anyway?

13

CHAPTER HIGHLIGHTS & NOTES: KEY TERMS, PEOPLE, PLACES, CONCEPTS

Caudate nucleus	The caudate nucleus is a nucleus located within the basal ganglia of the brains of many animal species. The caudate nucleus is an important part of the brain's learning and memory system. The caudate nuclei are located near the center of the brain, sitting astride the thalamus.
Morgan's Canon	Coined by 19th-century British psychologist C. Lloyd Morgan, Morgan's Canon remains a fundamental precept of comparative (animal) psychology. In its developed form it states that:In no case is an animal activity to be interpreted in terms of higher psychological processes, if it can be fairly interpreted in terms of processes which stand lower in the scale of psychological evolution and development. (Morgan 1903, p. 59) In other words we should only consider behaviour as, for example, rational, purposive or affectionate if there is no other explanation in terms of the behaviours of more primitive life-forms to which we do not attribute those faculties.
Scientific journal	In academic publishing, a scientific journal is a periodical publication intended to further the progress of science, usually by reporting new research. There are thousands of scientific journals in publication, and many more have been published at various points in the past . Most journals are highly specialized, although some of the oldest journals such as Nature publish articles and scientific papers across a wide range of scientific fields.
Leucotome	A leucotome is a surgical instrument used for performing leucotomies, lobotomies and other forms of psychosurgery. Invented by Canadian neurosurgeon Dr. Kenneth G. McKenzie in the 1940s, the leucotome has a narrow shaft which is inserted into the brain through a hole in the skull, and then a plunger on the back of the leucotome is depressed to extend a wire loop or metal strip into the brain. The leucotome is then rotated, cutting a core of brain tissue.
Lobotomy	Lobotomy (Greek: λοβ?ς - lobos: 'lobe (of brain)'; τομ? - tome: 'cut/slice') is a neurosurgical procedure, a form of psychosurgery, also known as a leukotomy or leucotomy . It consists of cutting the connections to and from the prefrontal cortex, the anterior part of the frontal lobes of the brain. While the procedure, initially termed a leucotomy, has been controversial since its inception in 1935, it was a mainstream procedure for more than two decades, prescribed for psychiatric (and occasionally other) conditions--this despite general recognition of frequent and serious side-effects.

Chapter 1. Biopsychology as a Neuroscience What Is Biopsychology, Anyway?

CHAPTER QUIZ: KEY TERMS, PEOPLE, PLACES, CONCEPTS

1. _____ is the study of the anatomy and stereotyped organization of nervous systems. In contrast to animals with radial symmetry, whose nervous system consists of a distributed network of cells, animals with bilateral symmetry have segregated, defined nervous systems, and thus we can make much more precise statements about their _____. In vertebrates, the nervous system is segregated into the internal structure of the brain and spinal cord (together called the central nervous system, or CNS) and the routes of the nerves that connect to the rest of the body (known as the peripheral nervous system, or PNS).

   a. Neuromorphology
   b. Neuron
   c. Neuroanatomy
   d. Nuclear chain fiber

2. _____ is a neurological disorder caused by the lack of thiamine (vitamin B_1) in the brain. Its onset is linked to chronic alcohol abuse and/or severe malnutrition. The syndrome is named after Sergei Korsakoff, the neuropsychiatrist who popularized the theory.

   a. Meige's syndrome
   b. Phantom eye syndrome
   c. Subclavian steal syndrome
   d. Korsakoff's syndrome

3. _____ is a peer-reviewed scientific journal in the field of neuroscience. It was established in 1962 as the International Journal of _____ and obtained its current name in 1970.

   a. Carl Rogers theory evaluation
   b. Neuropharmacology
   c. Neuroplasticity
   d. Neuropsychophysiology

4. In psychology and neuroscience, memory span is the longest list of items that a person can repeat back in correct order immediately after presentation on 50% of all trials. Items may include words, numbers, or letters. The task is known as _____ when numbers are used.

   a. Carl Rogers theory evaluation
   b. Digit Span
   c. Posse Comitatus Act
   d. Wilkinson v Downton

5. . _____, biopsychology, or psychobiology is the application of the principles of biology (in particular neurobiology), to the study of physiological, genetic, and developmental mechanisms of behavior in human and non-human animals. It typically investigates at the level of nerves, neurotransmitters, brain circuitry and the basic biological processes that underlie normal and abnormal behavior.

Chapter 1. Biopsychology as a Neuroscience What Is Biopsychology, Anyway?

15

Most typically, experiments in _____ involve non-human animal models (such as rats and mice, and non-human primates) which have implications for better understanding of human pathology and therefore contribute to evidence-based practice.

a. Behavioral neuroscience
b. Barry Everitt
c. Fear processing in the brain
d. Genes, Brain and Behavior

1. c
2. d
3. b
4. b
5. a

You can take the complete Chapter Practice Test

for Chapter 1. Biopsychology as a Neuroscience What Is Biopsychology, Anyway?
on all key terms, persons, places, and concepts.

Online 99 Cents

http://www.epub3.10.9241.1.cram101.com/

Use www.Cram101.com for all your study needs

including Cram101's online interactive problem solving labs in

chemistry, statistics, mathematics, and more.

	Behaviorism
	Renaissance
	Zeitgeist
	Self-awareness
	Natural selection
	Courtship display
	Dominance hierarchy
	Evolutionary psychology
	Exaptation
	Spandrel
	Polygyny
	Promiscuity
	Monogamy
	Polyandry
	Allele
	Mendelian inheritance
	Phenotype
	Gamete
	Meiosis

Chapter 2. Evolution, Genetics, and Experience
CHAPTER OUTLINE: KEY TERMS, PEOPLE, PLACES, CONCEPTS

Zygote

Linkage

Chromosomal crossover

Gene map

Down syndrome

Mutation

Mitochondria

Mitochondrial DNA

Transfer RNA

Ontogeny

Dopamine

Phenylketonuria

Tyrosine

Neurogenesis

Dizygotic twins

Intelligence quotient

Wechsler Adult Intelligence Scale

Behaviorism	Behaviorism also called the learning perspective (where any physical action is a behavior), is a philosophy of psychology based on the proposition that all things that organisms do--including acting, thinking and feeling--can and should be regarded as behaviors. The behaviorist school of thought maintains that behaviors as such can be described scientifically without recourse either to internal physiological events or to hypothetical constructs such as the mind. Behaviorism comprises the position that all theories should have observational correlates but that there are no philosophical differences between publicly observable processes (such as actions) and privately observable processes (such as thinking and feeling).
Renaissance	The Renaissance was a cultural movement that spanned the period roughly from the 14th to the 17th century, beginning in Italy in the Late Middle Ages and later spreading to the rest of Europe. Though availability of paper and the invention of metal movable type sped the dissemination of ideas from the later 15th century, the changes of the Renaissance were not uniformly experienced across Europe. As a cultural movement, it encompassed innovative flowering of Latin and vernacular literatures, beginning with the 14th-century resurgence of learning based on classical sources, which contemporaries credited to Petrarch, the development of linear perspective and other techniques of rendering a more natural reality in painting, and gradual but widespread educational reform.
Zeitgeist	Zeitgeist is 'the spirit of the times' or 'the spirit of the age.' Zeitgeist is the general cultural, intellectual, ethical, spiritual, or political climate within a nation or even specific groups, along with the general ambiance, morals, sociocultural direction, and mood associated with an era. The term is a loanword from German Zeit - 'time' and Geist - 'spirit' . Origins The concept of Zeitgeist goes back to Johann Gottfried Herder and other German Romanticists, such as Cornelius Jagdmann, but is best known in relation to Hegel's philosophy of history.
Self-awareness	Self-awareness is the capacity for introspection and the ability to reconcile oneself as an individual separate from the environment and other individuals. Self-awareness, though similar to sentience in concept, includes the experience of the self, and has been argued as implicit to the hard problem of consciousness. A philosophical view ''''' While reading Descartes, Locke began to relish the great ideas of philosophy and the scientific method.
Natural selection	Natural selection is the process by which traits become more or less common in a population due to consistent effects upon the survival or reproduction of their bearers. It is a key mechanism of evolution.

Chapter 2. Evolution, Genetics, and Experience

Courtship display	Courtship display is a special, sometimes ritualised, set of behaviours which some animals perform as part of courtship. Courtship behaviours can include special calls, postures, and movements, and may involve special plumage, bright colours or other ornamentation. A good example is the 'dancing' done by male birds of paradise.
Dominance hierarchy	A dominance hierarchy is the organization of individuals in a group that occurs when competition for resources leads to aggression. Schjelderup-Ebbe, who studied the often-cited example of the pecking order in chickens, found that such social structures lead to more stable flocks with reduced aggression among individuals. Dominance hierarchies can be despotic or linear.
Evolutionary psychology	Evolutionary psychology is an approach in the social and natural sciences that examines psychological traits such as memory, perception, and language from a modern evolutionary perspective. It seeks to identify which human psychological traits are evolved adaptations - that is, the functional products of natural selection or sexual selection. Adaptationist thinking about physiological mechanisms, such as the heart, lungs, and immune system, is common in evolutionary biology.
Exaptation	Exaptation, cooption, and preadaptation are related terms referring to shifts in the function of a trait during evolution. For example, a trait can evolve because it served one particular function, but subsequently it may come to serve another. Exaptations are common in both anatomy and behaviour.
Spandrel	In evolutionary biology, a Spandrel is a phenotypic characteristic that is a byproduct of the evolution of some other characteristic, rather than a direct product of adaptive selection. The term was coined by the Harvard paleontologist Stephen Jay Gould and population geneticist Richard Lewontin in their influential paper 'The Spandrels of San Marco and the Panglossian Paradigm: A Critique of the Adaptationist Programme' (1979). In this paper Gould and Lewontin employed the analogy of spandrels in Renaissance architecture: curved areas of masonry between arches supporting a dome that arise as a consequence of decisions about the shape of the arches and the base of the dome, rather than being designed for the artistic purposes for which they were often employed.
Polygyny	Polygyny is a form of marriage in which a man has two or more wives at the same time. In countries where the practice is illegal, the man is referred to as a bigamist or a polygamist.

Promiscuity	Promiscuity, in human sexual behavior, refers to the practice of casual sex with multiple sexual partners. The term can carry a moral judgement and is viewed in the context of the mainstream social ideal for sexual activity to take place within exclusive committed relationships. A common example of behavior viewed as promiscuous within the mainstream social ideals of many cultures is a one night stand.
Monogamy	Monogamy is a form of marriage in which an individual has only one spouse during their lifetime or at any one time (serial monogamy). In current usage, monogamy often refers to having one sexual partner irrespective of marriage or reproduction.
Polyandry	Polyandry refers to a form of marriage in which a woman has two or more husbands at the same time. The form of polyandry in which a woman is married to two or more brothers is known as 'fraternal polyandry', and it is believed by many anthropologists to be the most frequently encountered form. According to inscriptions describing the reforms of the Sumerian king Urukagina of Lagash (ca. 2300 BC), he is said to have abolished the former custom of polyandry in his country, on pain of the woman taking multiple husbands being stoned with rocks upon which her crime is written.
Allele	An allele is one of two or more forms of a gene or a genetic locus (generally a group of genes). The form 'allel' is also used, an abbreviation of allelomorph. Sometimes, different alleles can result in different observable phenotypic traits, such as different pigmentation.
Mendelian inheritance	Mendelian inheritance, hereditary characteristics from parent organisms to their offspring; it underlies much of genetics. They were initially derived from the work of Gregor Johann Mendel published in 1865 and 1866 which was 're-discovered' in 1900, and were initially very controversial. When they were integrated with the chromosome theory of inheritance by Thomas Hunt Morgan in 1915, they became the core of classical genetics.
Phenotype	A phenotype is any observable characteristic or trait of an organism: such as its morphology, development, biochemical or physiological properties, behavior, and products of behavior (such as a bird's nest). Phenotypes result from the expression of an organism's genes as well as the influence of environmental factors and the interactions between the two.
Gamete	A gamete is a cell that fuses with another cell during fertilization (conception) in organisms that reproduce sexually. In species that produce two morphologically distinct types of gametes, and in which each individual produces only one type, a female is any individual that produces the larger type of gamete--called an ovum (or egg)--and a male produces the smaller tadpole-like type--called a sperm.

Chapter 2. Evolution, Genetics, and Experience

Meiosis	In rhetoric, meiosis is a euphemistic figure of speech that intentionally understates something or implies that it is lesser in significance or size than it really is. Meiosis is the opposite of auxesis, and also sometimes used as a synonym for litotes. The term is derived from the Greek μει?ω ('to make smaller', 'to diminish').
Zygote	A zygote is the initial cell formed when a new organism is produced by means of sexual reproduction. A zygote is synthesized from the union of two gametes, and constitutes the first stage in a unique organism's development. Zygotes are usually produced by a fertilization event between two haploid cells--an ovum from a female and a sperm cell from a male--which combine to form the single diploid cell.
Linkage	In linguistics, a linkage is a group of undoubtedly related languages for which no proto-language can be reconstructed. Malcolm Ross, who coined the term, defined it as 'a group of communalects which have arisen by dialect differentiation' (Ross 1988, p. 8). Common to linkages are defining features absent from its geographic extremes.
Chromosomal crossover	Chromosomal crossover is an exchange of genetic material between homologous chromosomes. It is one of the final phases of genetic recombination, which occurs during prophase I of meiosis (pachytene) in a process called synapsis. Synapsis begins before the synaptonemal complex develops, and is not completed until near the end of prophase I. Crossover usually occurs when matching regions on matching chromosomes break and then reconnect to the other chromosome.
Gene map	A gene map is the descriptive representation of the structure of a single gene. It includes the DNA sequence of a gene with introns and exons, 3' or 5' transcribed-untranslated regions, termination (poly-adenylation) signal, regulatory elements such as promoters, enhancers and it may include known mutations defining alternative alleles of the same gene.
Down syndrome	Down syndrome, also known as trisomy 21, is a chromosomal condition caused by the presence of all or part of a third copy of chromosome 21. Down syndrome is the most common chromosome abnormality in humans. It is typically associated with a delay in cognitive ability (mental retardation, or MR) and physical growth, and a particular set of facial characteristics. The average IQ of young adults with Down syndrome is around 50, compared to children without the condition with an IQ of 100. (MR has historically been defined as an IQ below 70).
Mutation	In molecular biology and genetics, mutations are changes in a genomic sequence: the DNA sequence of a cell's genome or the DNA or RNA sequence of a virus. These random sequences can be defined as sudden and spontaneous changes in the cell.

Mitochondria	Mitochondria are membrane-enclosed organelle found in most eukaryotic cells. These organelles range from 0.5 to 1.0 micrometer (μm) in diameter. Mitochondria are sometimes described as 'cellular power plants' because they generate most of the cell's supply of adenosine triphosphate (ATP), used as a source of chemical energy.
Mitochondrial DNA	Mitochondrial DNA is the DNA located in organelles called mitochondria, structures within eukaryotic cells that convert the chemical energy from food into a form that cells can use, ATP. Most other DNA present in eukaryotic organisms is found in the cell nucleus.
Transfer RNA	Transfer RNA is an adaptor molecule composed of RNA, typically 73 to 93 nucleotides in length, that is used in biology to bridge the three-letter genetic code in messenger RNA (mRNA) with the twenty-letter code of amino acids in proteins. The role of tRNA as an adaptor is best understood by considering its three-dimensional structure. One end of the tRNA carries the genetic code in a three-nucleotide sequence called the anticodon.
Ontogeny	Ontogeny (also ontogenesis or morphogenesis) is the origin and the development of an organism - for example: from the fertilized egg to mature form. It covers in essence, the study of an organism's lifespan. The word 'ontogeny' comes from the Greek ?ντος, ontos, present participle singular of ε?ναι, 'to be'; and from the suffix -geny, which expresses the concept of 'mode of production'.
Dopamine	Dopamine, a simple organic chemical in the catecholamine family, plays a number of important physiological roles in the bodies of animals. Its name derives from its chemical structure, which consists of an amine group (NH_2) linked to a catechol structure called dihydroxyphenethylamine, the decarboxyalted form of dihydroxyphenylalanine (acronym DOPA). In the brain, dopamine functions as a neurotransmitter--a chemical released by nerve cells to send signals to other nerve cells.
Phenylketonuria	Phenylketonuria is an autosomal recessive metabolic genetic disorder characterized by a mutation in the gene for the hepatic enzyme phenylalanine hydroxylase (PAH), rendering it nonfunctional. This enzyme is necessary to metabolize the amino acid phenylalanine (Phe) to the amino acid tyrosine. When PAH activity is reduced, phenylalanine accumulates and is converted into phenylpyruvate (also known as phenylketone), which is detected in the urine.
Tyrosine	Tyrosine or 4-hydroxyphenylalanine, is one of the 22 amino acids that are used by cells to synthesize proteins. Its codons are UAC and UAU. It is a non-essential amino acid with a polar side group. The word 'tyrosine' is from the Greek tyri, meaning cheese, as it was first discovered in 1846 by German chemist Justus von Liebig in the protein casein from cheese.
Neurogenesis	Neurogenesis is the process by which neurons are generated from neural stem and progenitor cells.

Chapter 2. Evolution, Genetics, and Experience

	Most active during pre-natal development, neurogenesis is responsible for populating the growing brain with neurons. Recently neurogenesis was shown to continue in several small parts of the brain of mammals: the hippocampus and the subventricular zone.
Dizygotic twins	Dizygotic twins usually occur when two fertilized eggs are implanted in the uterus wall at the same time. When two eggs are independently fertilized by two different sperm cells, fraternal twins result. The two eggs, or ova, form two zygotes, hence the terms dizygotic and biovular.
Intelligence quotient	An intelligence quotient, is a score derived from one of several standardized tests designed to assess intelligence. The abbreviation 'IQ' comes from the German term Intelligenz-Quotient, originally coined by psychologist William Stern. When modern IQ tests are devised, the mean (average) score within an age group is set to 100 and the standard deviation (SD) almost always to 15, although this was not always so historically.
Wechsler Adult Intelligence Scale	The Wechsler Adult Intelligence Scale is a test designed to measure intelligence in adults and older adolescents. It is currently in its fourth edition (WAIS-IV). The original WAIS (Form I) was published in February 1955 by David Wechsler, as a revision of the Wechsler-Bellevue Intelligence Scale.

1. An _____, is a score derived from one of several standardized tests designed to assess intelligence. The abbreviation 'IQ' comes from the German term Intelligenz-Quotient, originally coined by psychologist William Stern. When modern IQ tests are devised, the mean (average) score within an age group is set to 100 and the standard deviation (SD) almost always to 15, although this was not always so historically.

    a. International Society for Intelligence Research
    b. Intelligence quotient
    c. U.S. Presidential IQ hoax
    d. Organized Crime Control Act

2. . _____, a simple organic chemical in the catecholamine family, plays a number of important physiological roles in the bodies of animals. Its name derives from its chemical structure, which consists of an amine group (NH_2) linked to a catechol structure called dihydroxyphenethylamine, the decarboxyalted form of dihydroxyphenylalanine (acronym DOPA). In the brain, _____ functions as a neurotransmitter--a chemical released by nerve cells to send signals to other nerve cells.

    a. Dopaminergic
    b. Dynorphin

c. False neurotransmitter

d. Dopamine

3. _____ refers to a form of marriage in which a woman has two or more husbands at the same time. The form of _____ in which a woman is married to two or more brothers is known as 'fraternal _____', and it is believed by many anthropologists to be the most frequently encountered form. Human _____

According to inscriptions describing the reforms of the Sumerian king Urukagina of Lagash (ca. 2300 BC), he is said to have abolished the former custom of _____ in his country, on pain of the woman taking multiple husbands being stoned with rocks upon which her crime is written.

a. Polygamy

b. Polygyny threshold model

c. Polyandry

d. Mating system

4. A _____ is the initial cell formed when a new organism is produced by means of sexual reproduction. A _____ is synthesized from the union of two gametes, and constitutes the first stage in a unique organism's development. _____s are usually produced by a fertilization event between two haploid cells--an ovum from a female and a sperm cell from a male--which combine to form the single diploid cell.

a. Bidder's organ

b. Blood-testis barrier

c. Zygote

d. Cortical reaction

5. _____ is a form of marriage in which a man has two or more wives at the same time. In countries where the practice is illegal, the man is referred to as a bigamist or a polygamist. It is distinguished from relationships where a man has a sexual partner outside marriage, such as a concubine, casual sexual partner, paramour, cohabits with a married woman or other culturally but not legally recognized secondary partner.

a. Poppet

b. Postmodernist anthropology

c. Polygyny

d. Predmost 3

1. b
2. d
3. c
4. c
5. c

You can take the complete Chapter Practice Test

for Chapter 2. Evolution, Genetics, and Experience
on all key terms, persons, places, and concepts.

Online 99 Cents

http://www.epub3.10.9241.2.cram101.com/

Use www.Cram101.com for all your study needs

including Cram101's online interactive problem solving labs in

chemistry, statistics, mathematics, and more.

Chapter 3. The Anatomy of the Nervous System

CHAPTER OUTLINE: KEY TERMS, PEOPLE, PLACES, CONCEPTS

_____ Autonomic nervous system

_____ Central nervous system

_____ Peripheral nervous system

_____ Somatic nervous system

_____ Spinal cord

_____ Cerebral aqueduct

_____ Cerebrospinal fluid

_____ Hydrocephalus

_____ Glial cell

_____ Axon

_____ Axon hillock

_____ Dendrite

_____ Myelin

_____ Microtubule

_____ Mitochondria

_____ Neurotransmitter

_____ Synaptic vesicle

_____ Interneuron

_____ Multipolar neuron

CHAPTER OUTLINE: KEY TERMS, PEOPLE, PLACES, CONCEPTS

Astrocyte

Oligodendrocyte

Schwann cell

Microglia

Neuroanatomy

Neuron

Scanning electron microscope

Electron microscope

Nervous system

Cerebral hemisphere

Mesencephalon

Metencephalon

Cerebrum

Cerebellum

Tegmentum

Hypothalamus

Periaqueductal gray

Red nucleus

Substantia nigra

Thalamus

Ventral posterior nucleus

Cerebral cortex

Corpus callosum

Gyrus

Occipital lobe

Optic chiasm

Optic nerve

Parietal lobe

Pituitary gland

Temporal lobe

Apical dendrite

Neocortex

Stellate cell

Hippocampus

Limbic system

Amygdala

Cingulate cortex

Parkinson's disease

	Basal ganglia

	Dendritic spine

CHAPTER HIGHLIGHTS & NOTES: KEY TERMS, PEOPLE, PLACES, CONCEPTS

Autonomic nervous system	The autonomic nervous system is the part of the peripheral nervous system that acts as a control system functioning largely below the level of consciousness, and controls visceral functions. The Autonomic nervous system affects heart rate, digestion, respiration rate, salivation, perspiration, diameter of the pupils, micturition (urination), and sexual arousal. Whereas most of its actions are involuntary, some, such as breathing, work in tandem with the conscious mind.
Central nervous system	The central nervous system is the part of the nervous system that integrates the information that it receives from, and coordinates the activity of, all parts of the bodies of bilaterian animals-that is, all multicellular animals except radially symmetric animals such as sponges and jellyfish. It contains the majority of the nervous system and consists of the brain and the spinal cord. Some classifications also include the retina and the cranial nerves in the Central nervous system. Together with the peripheral nervous system, it has a fundamental role in the control of behavior.
Peripheral nervous system	The peripheral nervous system consists of the nerves and ganglia outside of the brain and spinal cord. The main function of the Peripheral nervous system is to connect the central nervous system (CNS) to the limbs and organs. Unlike the CNS, the Peripheral nervous system is not protected by the bone of spine and skull, or by the blood-brain barrier, leaving it exposed to toxins and mechanical injuries.
Somatic nervous system	The somatic nervous system is the part of the peripheral nervous system associated with the voluntary control of body movements via skeletal muscles. The SoNS consists of efferent nerves responsible for stimulating muscle contraction, including all the non-sensory neurons connected with skeletal muscles and skin. Parts of Somatic Nervous System There are 43 segments of nerves in our body and with each segment there is a pair of sensory and motor nerves.

Chapter 3. The Anatomy of the Nervous System

Spinal cord	The spinal cord is a long, thin, tubular bundle of nervous tissue and support cells that extends from the brain (the medulla oblongata specifically). The brain and spinal cord together make up the central nervous system (CNS). The spinal cord begins at the occipital bone and extends down to the space between the first and second lumbar vertebrae; it does not extend the entire length of the vertebral column.
Cerebral aqueduct	The mesencephalic duct, also known as the aqueductus mesencephali, aqueduct of Sylvius or the cerebral aqueduct, contains cerebrospinal fluid (CSF), is within the mesencephalon and connects the third ventricle in the diencephalon to the fourth ventricle within the region of the mesencephalon and metencephalon, located dorsal to the pons and ventral to the cerebellum.

The cerebral aqueduct, similarly to other parts of the ventricular system of the brain, develops from the central canal of the neural tube. Specifically, the duct originates from the portion of the neural tube that is present in the developing mesencephalon, hence the name 'mesencephalic duct.' Pathology

A blockage in this duct is a cause of hydrocephalus. |
| Cerebrospinal fluid | Cerebrospinal fluid Liquor cerebrospinalis, is a clear, colorless, bodily fluid, that occupies the subarachnoid space and the ventricular system around and inside the brain and spinal cord.

The CSF occupies the space between the arachnoid mater (the middle layer of the brain cover, meninges) and the pia mater (the layer of the meninges closest to the brain). It constitutes the content of all intra-cerebral (inside the brain, cerebrum) ventricles, cisterns, and sulci, as well as the central canal of the spinal cord. |
Hydrocephalus	Hydrocephalus also known as 'water on the brain,' is a medical condition in which there is an abnormal accumulation of cerebrospinal fluid (CSF) in the ventricles, or cavities, of the brain. This may cause increased intracranial pressure inside the skull and progressive enlargement of the head, convulsion, tunnel vision, and mental disability. Hydrocephalus can also cause death.
Glial cell	Glial cells are non-neuronal cells that maintain homeostasis, form myelin, and provide support and protection for the brain's neurons. In the human brain, there is roughly one glia for every neuron with a ratio of about two neurons for every three glia in the cerebral gray matter.
Axon	An axon is a long, slender projection of a nerve cell, or neuron, that typically conducts electrical impulses away from the neuron's cell body. In certain sensory neurons (pseudounipolar neurons), such as those for touch and warmth, the electrical impulse travels along an axon from the periphery to the cell body, and from the cell body to the spinal cord along another branch of the same axon.

Axon hillock	The axon hillock is a specialized part of the cell body (or soma) of a neuron that connects to the axon. As a result, the axon hillock is the last site in the soma where membrane potentials propagated from synaptic inputs are summated before being transmitted to the axon. For many years, it had been believed that the axon hillock was the usual site of action potential initiation.
Dendrite	Dendrites are the branched projections of a neuron that act to conduct the electrochemical stimulation received from other neural cells to the cell body, or soma, of the neuron from which the dendrites project. Electrical stimulation is transmitted onto dendrites by upstream neurons via synapses which are located at various points throughout the dendritic arbor. Dendrites play a critical role in integrating these synaptic inputs and in determining the extent to which action potentials are produced by the neuron.
Myelin	Myelin is a dielectric material that forms a layer, the myelin sheath, usually around only the axon of a neuron. It is essential for the proper functioning of the nervous system. Myelin is an outgrowth of a type of glial cell.
Microtubule	Microtubules are one of the active matter components of the cytoskeleton. They have a diameter of 25 nm and length varying from 200 nanometers to 25 micrometers. Microtubules serve as structural components within cells and are involved in many cellular processes including mitosis, cytokinesis, and vesicular transport.
Mitochondria	Mitochondria are membrane-enclosed organelle found in most eukaryotic cells. These organelles range from 0.5 to 1.0 micrometer (μm) in diameter. Mitochondria are sometimes described as 'cellular power plants' because they generate most of the cell's supply of adenosine triphosphate (ATP), used as a source of chemical energy.
Neurotransmitter	Neurotransmitters are endogenous chemicals that transmit signals from a neuron to a target cell across a synapse. Neurotransmitters are packaged into synaptic vesicles clustered beneath the membrane in the axon terminal, on the presynaptic side of a synapse. They are released into and diffuse across the synaptic cleft, where they bind to specific receptors in the membrane on the postsynaptic side of the synapse.
Synaptic vesicle	In a neuron, synaptic vesicles store various neurotransmitters that are released at the synapse. The release is regulated by a voltage-dependent calcium channel. Vesicles are essential for propagating nerve impulses between neurons and are constantly recreated by the cell.
Interneuron	An interneuron is a neuron that forms a connection between other neurons. Interneurons are neither motor nor sensory. The term is also applied to brain and spinal cord neurons whose axons connect only with nearby neurons, to distinguish them from 'projection' neurons, whose axons (projection fibers) project to more distant regions of the brain or spinal cord.

Chapter 3. The Anatomy of the Nervous System

Multipolar neuron	A multipolar neuron is a type of neuron that possesses a single (usually long) axon and many dendrites, allowing for the integration of a great deal of information from other neurons. These dendritic branches can also emerge from the nerve cell body. Multipolar neurons constitute the majority of neurons in the brain and include motor neurons and interneurons.
Astrocyte	Astrocytes (etymology: astron gk. star, cyte gk. cell), also known collectively as astroglia, are characteristic star-shaped glial cells in the brain and spinal cord.
Oligodendrocyte	An oligodendrocyte are a type of brain cell. They are a variety of neuroglia. Their main functions are to provide support and to insulate the axons (the long projection of nerve cells) in the central nervous system (the brain and spinal cord) of some vertebrates.
Schwann cell	Schwann cells or neurolemmocytes are the principal glia of the peripheral nervous system (PNS). Glial cells function to support neurons and in the PNS, also include satellite cells, olfactory ensheathing cells, enteric glia and glia that reside at sensory nerve endings, such as the Pacinian corpuscle. There are two types of Schwann cell, myelinating and nonmyelinating.
Microglia	Microglia are a type of glial cell that are the resident macrophages of the brain and spinal cord, and thus act as the first and main form of active immune defense in the central nervous system (CNS). Microglia constitute 20% of the total glial cell population within the brain. Microglia are distributed in large non-overlapping regions throughout the brain and spinal cord.
Neuroanatomy	Neuroanatomy is the study of the anatomy and stereotyped organization of nervous systems. In contrast to animals with radial symmetry, whose nervous system consists of a distributed network of cells, animals with bilateral symmetry have segregated, defined nervous systems, and thus we can make much more precise statements about their neuroanatomy. In vertebrates, the nervous system is segregated into the internal structure of the brain and spinal cord (together called the central nervous system, or CNS) and the routes of the nerves that connect to the rest of the body (known as the peripheral nervous system, or PNS).
Neuron	A neuron is an electrically excitable cell that processes and transmits information through electrical and chemical signals. A chemical signal occurs via a synapse, a specialized connection with other cells. Neurons connect to each other to form neural networks.
Scanning electron microscope	A scanning electron microscope is a type of electron microscope that images a sample by scanning it with a high-energy beam of electrons in a raster scan pattern. The electrons interact with the atoms that make up the sample producing signals that contain information about the sample's surface topography, composition, and other properties such as electrical conductivity.

Chapter 3. The Anatomy of the Nervous System

Electron microscope	An electron microscope is a type of microscope that uses a beam of electrons to illuminate the specimen and produce a magnified image. Electron microscopes (EM) have a greater resolving power than a light-powered optical microscope, because electrons have wavelengths about 100,000 times shorter than visible light (photons), and can achieve better than 50 pm resolution and magnifications of up to about 10,000,000x, whereas ordinary, non-confocal light microscopes are limited by diffraction to about 200 nm resolution and useful magnifications below 2000x. The electron microscope uses electrostatic and electromagnetic 'lenses' to control the electron beam and focus it to form an image.
Nervous system	The nervous system is the part of an animal's body that coordinates the actions of the animal and transmits signals between different parts of its body. In most types of animal it consists of two parts, the central nervous system and peripheral nervous system. The CNS contains the brain and spinal cord.
Cerebral hemisphere	A cerebral hemisphere is one of the two regions of the eutherian brain that are delineated by the median plane, (medial longitudinal fissure). The brain can thus be described as being divided into left and right cerebral hemispheres. Each of these hemispheres has an outer layer of grey matter called the cerebral cortex that is supported by an inner layer of white matter.
Mesencephalon	In biological anatomy, the mesencephalon (or midbrain) comprises the tectum (or corpora quadrigemina), tegmentum, the ventricular mesocoelia (or 'iter'), and the cerebral peduncles, as well as several nuclei and fasciculi. Caudally the mesencephalon adjoins the pons (metencephalon) and rostrally it adjoins the diencephalon (Thalamus, hypothalamus, et al).. During development, the mesencephalon forms from the middle of three vesicles that arise from the neural tube to generate the brain.
Metencephalon	The metencephalon is a developmental categorization of portions of the central nervous system. The metencephalon is composed of the pons and the cerebellum; contains a portion of the fourth ventricle; and the trigeminal nerve (CN V), abducens nerve (CN VI), facial nerve (CN VII), and a portion of the vestibulocochlear nerve (CN VIII). The metencephalon develops from the higher/rostral half of the embryonic rhombencephalon, and is differentiated from the myelencephalon in the embryo by approximately 5 weeks of age.
Cerebrum	The cerebrum, together with the diencephalon, constitutes the forebrain. In humans, the cerebrum is the most superior region of the vertebrate central nervous system.

Chapter 3. The Anatomy of the Nervous System

Cerebellum	The cerebellum is a region of the brain that plays an important role in motor control. It is also involved in some cognitive functions such as attention and language, and probably in some emotional functions such as regulating fear and pleasure responses. Its movement-related functions are the most clearly understood, however.
Tegmentum	The tegmentum is a general area within the brainstem. It is located between the ventricular system and distinctive basal or ventral structures at each level. It forms the floor of the midbrain whereas the tectum forms the ceiling.
Hypothalamus	The Hypothalamus is a portion of the brain that contains a number of small nuclei with a variety of functions. One of the most important functions of the hypothalamus is to link the nervous system to the endocrine system via the pituitary gland (hypophysis). The hypothalamus is located below the thalamus, just above the brain stem.
Periaqueductal gray	Periaqueductal gray is the gray matter located around the cerebral aqueduct within the tegmentum of the midbrain. It plays a role in the descending modulation of pain and in defensive behaviour. The ascending pain and temperature fibers of the spinothalamic tract also send information to the PAG via the spinomesencephalic tract .
Red nucleus	The red nucleus is a structure in the rostral midbrain involved in motor coordination. It comprises a caudal magnocellular and a rostral parvocellular part. It is located in the tegmentum of the midbrain next to the substantia nigra.
Substantia nigra	The substantia nigra is a brain structure located in the mesencephalon (midbrain) that plays an important role in reward, addiction, and movement. Substantia nigra is Latin for 'black substance', as parts of the substantia nigra appear darker than neighboring areas due to high levels of melanin in dopaminergic neurons. Parkinson's disease is caused by the death of dopaminergic neurons in the substantia nigra pars compacta.
Thalamus	The thalamus is a midline symmetrical structure within the brains of vertebrates including humans, situated between the cerebral cortex and midbrain. Its function includes relaying sensory and motor signals to the cerebral cortex, along with the regulation of consciousness, sleep, and alertness. The thalamus surrounds the third ventricle.
Ventral posterior nucleus	The ventral posterior nucleus is the somato-sensory relay nucleus in thalamus of the brain. Input and output The ventral posterior nucleus receives neuronal input from the medial lemniscus, spinal lemniscus, spinothalamic tracts, and trigeminothalamic tract.

Chapter 3. The Anatomy of the Nervous System

Cerebral cortex	The cerebral cortex is a sheet of neural tissue that is outermost to the cerebrum of the mammalian brain. It plays a key role in memory, attention, perceptual awareness, thought, language, and consciousness. It is constituted of up to six horizontal layers, each of which has a different composition in terms of neurons and connectivity.
Corpus callosum	The corpus callosum, is a wide, flat bundle of neural fibers beneath the cortex in the eutherian brain at the longitudinal fissure. It connects the left and right cerebral hemispheres and facilitates interhemispheric communication. It is the largest white matter structure in the brain, consisting of 200-250 million contralateral axonal projections.
Gyrus	A gyrus is a ridge on the cerebral cortex. It is generally surrounded by one or more sulci (sl.
Occipital lobe	The occipital lobe is the visual processing center of the mammalian brain containing most of the anatomical region of the visual cortex. The primary visual cortex is Brodmann area 17, commonly called V1 (visual one). Human V1 is located on the medial side of the occipital lobe within the calcarine sulcus; the full extent of V1 often continues onto the posterior pole of the occipital lobe.
Optic chiasm	The optic chiasm is the part of the brain where the optic nerves (CN II) partially cross. The optic chiasm is located at the bottom of the brain immediately below the hypothalamus. The images on the nasal sides of each retina cross over to the opposite side of the brain via the optic nerve at the optic chiasm.
Optic nerve	The optic nerve, transmits visual information from the retina to the brain. Derived from the embryonic retinal ganglion cell, a diverticulum located in the diencephalon, the optic nerve does not regenerate after transection. The optic nerve is the second of twelve paired cranial nerves but is considered to be part of the central nervous system, as it is derived from an outpouching of the diencephalon during embryonic development.
Parietal lobe	The parietal lobe is a part of the brain positioned above (superior to) the occipital lobe and behind (posterior to) the frontal lobe. The parietal lobe integrates sensory information from different modalities, particularly determining spatial sense and navigation. For example, it comprises somatosensory cortex and the dorsal stream of the visual system.
Pituitary gland	In vertebrate anatomy the pituitary gland, is an endocrine gland about the size of a pea and weighing 0.5 g (0.02 oz)., in humans.

	It is a protrusion off the bottom of the hypothalamus at the base of the brain, and rests in a small, bony cavity (sella turcica) covered by a dural fold (diaphragma sellae). The pituitary is functionally connected to the hypothalamus by the median eminence via a small tube called the infundibular stem (Pituitary Stalk).
Temporal lobe	The temporal lobe is a region of the cerebral cortex that is located beneath the Sylvian fissure on both cerebral hemispheres of the mammalian brain. The temporal lobe is involved in auditory perception and is home to the primary auditory cortex. It is also important for the processing of semantics in both speech and vision. The temporal lobe contains the hippocampus and plays a key role in the formation of long-term memory.
Apical dendrite	An apical dendrite is a dendrite that emerges from the apex of a pyramidal cell. Apical dendrites are one of two primary categories of dendrites, and they distinguish the pyramidal cells from spiny stellate cells in the cortices. Pyramidal cells are found in the prefrontal cortex, the hippocampus, the entorhinal cortex, and the olfactory cortex.
Neocortex	The neocortex, is a part of the brain of mammals. It is the outer layer of the cerebral hemispheres, and made up of six layers, labelled I to VI (with VI being the innermost and I being the outermost). The neocortex is part of the cerebral cortex (along with the archicortex and paleocortex, which are cortical parts of the limbic system).
Stellate cell	In neuroscience, stellate cells are neurons with several dendrites radiating from the cell body giving them a star shaped why. The three most common stellate cells are the inhibitory interneurons found within the molecular layer of the cerebellum, excitatory spiny stellate interneurons and inhibitory aspiny stellate interneurons. Cerebellar stellate cells synapse onto the dendritic arbors of Purkinje cells.
Hippocampus	The hippocampus is a major component of the brains of humans and other mammals. It belongs to the limbic system and plays important roles in long-term memory and spatial navigation. Like the cerebral cortex, with which it is closely associated, it is a paired structure, with mirror-image halves in the left and right sides of the brain. In humans and other primates, the hippocampus is located inside the medial temporal lobe, beneath the cortical surface. It contains two main interlocking parts: Ammon's horn and the dentate gyrus.
Limbic system	The limbic system is a set of brain structures, including the hippocampus, amygdalae, anterior thalamic nuclei, septum, limbic cortex and fornix, which seemingly support a variety of functions including emotion, behavior, motivation, long-term memory, and olfaction. Etymology The term 'limbic' comes from the Latin limbus, for 'border' or 'edge'. Anatomy

Amygdala	The are almond-shaped groups of nuclei located deep within the medial temporal lobes of the brain in complex vertebrates, including humans. Shown in research to perform a primary role in the processing of memory and emotional reactions, the amygdalae are considered part of the limbic system. Anatomical subdivisions The regions described as amygdala nuclei encompass several structures with distinct connectional and functional characteristics in animals and humans.
Cingulate cortex	The cingulate cortex is a part of the brain situated in the medial aspect of the cortex. It includes the cortex of the cingulate gyrus, which lies immediately above the corpus callosum, and the continuation of this in the cingulate sulcus. The cingulate cortex is usually considered part of the limbic lobe.
Parkinson's disease	Parkinson's disease is a degenerative disorder of the central nervous system. It results from the death of dopamine-containing cells in the substantia nigra, a region of the midbrain; the cause of cell-death is unknown. Early in the course of the disease, the most obvious symptoms are movement-related, including shaking, rigidity, slowness of movement and difficulty with walking and gait. Later, cognitive and behavioural problems may arise, with dementia commonly occurring in the advanced stages of the disease. Other symptoms include sensory, sleep and emotional problems. Parkinson's disease is more common in the elderly with most cases occurring after the age of 50.
Basal ganglia	The basal ganglia are a group of nuclei of varied origin in the brains of vertebrates that act as a cohesive functional unit. They are situated at the base of the forebrain and are strongly connected with the cerebral cortex, thalamus and other brain areas. The basal ganglia are associated with a variety of functions, including voluntary motor control, procedural learning relating to routine behaviors or 'habits' such as bruxism, eye movements, and cognitive, emotional functions.
Dendritic spine	A dendritic spine is a small membranous protrusion from a neuron's dendrite that typically receives input from a single synapse of an axon. Dendritic spines serve as a storage site for synaptic strength and help transmit electrical signals to the neuron's cell body. Most spines have a bulbous head (the spine head), and a thin neck that connects the head of the spine to the shaft of the dendrite.

Chapter 3. The Anatomy of the Nervous System

1. The _____, transmits visual information from the retina to the brain. Derived from the embryonic retinal ganglion cell, a diverticulum located in the diencephalon, the _____ does not regenerate after transection.

    The _____ is the second of twelve paired cranial nerves but is considered to be part of the central nervous system, as it is derived from an outpouching of the diencephalon during embryonic development.

    a. Optic tract
    b. Optokinetic reflex
    c. Optic tract
    d. Optic nerve

2. The _____ is a structure in the rostral midbrain involved in motor coordination. It comprises a caudal magnocellular and a rostral parvocellular part. It is located in the tegmentum of the midbrain next to the substantia nigra.

    a. Carl Rogers theory evaluation
    b. Red nucleus
    c. Hypothalamic-pituitary-adrenal axis
    d. Supraoptic nucleus

3. The _____ is a long, thin, tubular bundle of nervous tissue and support cells that extends from the brain (the medulla oblongata specifically). The brain and _____ together make up the central nervous system (CNS). The _____ begins at the occipital bone and extends down to the space between the first and second lumbar vertebrae; it does not extend the entire length of the vertebral column.

    a. Survival of motor neuron
    b. Spinal cord
    c. Vestibulospinal tract
    d. Rubrospinal tract

4. _____s or neurolemmocytes are the principal glia of the peripheral nervous system (PNS). Glial cells function to support neurons and in the PNS, also include satellite cells, olfactory ensheathing cells, enteric glia and glia that reside at sensory nerve endings, such as the Pacinian corpuscle. There are two types of _____, myelinating and nonmyelinating.

    a. Seizure prediction
    b. Sensory gating
    c. Schwann cell
    d. Shunting

5. . The _____ is a sheet of neural tissue that is outermost to the cerebrum of the mammalian brain. It plays a key role in memory, attention, perceptual awareness, thought, language, and consciousness. It is constituted of up to six horizontal layers, each of which has a different composition in terms of neurons and connectivity.

    a. allocortex

b. Cerebral cortex

c. Merighi

d. Gregory Berns

1. d
2. b
3. b
4. c
5. b

You can take the complete Chapter Practice Test

for Chapter 3. The Anatomy of the Nervous System
on all key terms, persons, places, and concepts.

Online 99 Cents

http://www.epub3.10.9241.3.cram101.com/

Use www.Cram101.com for all your study needs

including Cram101's online interactive problem solving labs in

chemistry, statistics, mathematics, and more.

Chapter 4. Neural Conduction and Synaptic Transmission

CHAPTER OUTLINE: KEY TERMS, PEOPLE, PLACES, CONCEPTS

Parkinson's disease

Substantia nigra

Ion channel

Dendrite

Depolarization

Excitatory postsynaptic potential

Hyperpolarization

Inhibitory postsynaptic potential

Neurotransmitter

Action potential

Axon hillock

Refractory period

Interneuron

Myelin

Saltatory conduction

Compartmentalization

Dendritic spine

Neurotransmission

Microtubule

_____ | Ligand

_____ | Receptor

_____ | Autoreceptor

_____ | G protein

_____ | Metabotropic receptor

_____ | Second messenger

_____ | Reuptake

_____ | Acetylcholine

_____ | Acetylcholinesterase

_____ | Astrocyte

_____ | Electrical synapse

_____ | Carbon monoxide

_____ | Catecholamine

_____ | Dopamine

_____ | Epinephrine

_____ | Indolamines

_____ | Norepinephrine

_____ | Serotonin

_____ | Tyrosine

Chapter 4. Neural Conduction and Synaptic Transmission

CHAPTER OUTLINE: KEY TERMS, PEOPLE, PLACES, CONCEPTS

_______________ Endorphin

_______________ Neuropeptide

_______________ Agonist

_______________ Cocaine

_______________ Synaptic vesicle

_______________ Psychoactive drug

_______________ Anticonvulsant

_______________ Anxiolytic

_______________ Benzodiazepine

_______________ Chlordiazepoxide

_______________ Diazepam

_______________ Sedative

Chapter 4. Neural Conduction and Synaptic Transmission

Parkinson's disease	Parkinson's disease is a degenerative disorder of the central nervous system. It results from the death of dopamine-containing cells in the substantia nigra, a region of the midbrain; the cause of cell-death is unknown. Early in the course of the disease, the most obvious symptoms are movement-related, including shaking, rigidity, slowness of movement and difficulty with walking and gait. Later, cognitive and behavioural problems may arise, with dementia commonly occurring in the advanced stages of the disease. Other symptoms include sensory, sleep and emotional problems. Parkinson's disease is more common in the elderly with most cases occurring after the age of 50.
Substantia nigra	The substantia nigra is a brain structure located in the mesencephalon (midbrain) that plays an important role in reward, addiction, and movement. Substantia nigra is Latin for 'black substance', as parts of the substantia nigra appear darker than neighboring areas due to high levels of melanin in dopaminergic neurons. Parkinson's disease is caused by the death of dopaminergic neurons in the substantia nigra pars compacta.
Ion channel	Ion channels are pore-forming proteins that help establish and control the voltage gradient across the plasma membrane of cells by allowing the flow of ions down their electrochemical gradient. They are present in the membranes that surround all biological cells. The study of ion channels involves many scientific techniques such as voltage clamp electrophysiology (in particular patch clamp), immunohistochemistry, and RT-PCR. Ion channels regulate the flow of ions across the membrane in all cells.
Dendrite	Dendrites are the branched projections of a neuron that act to conduct the electrochemical stimulation received from other neural cells to the cell body, or soma, of the neuron from which the dendrites project. Electrical stimulation is transmitted onto dendrites by upstream neurons via synapses which are located at various points throughout the dendritic arbor. Dendrites play a critical role in integrating these synaptic inputs and in determining the extent to which action potentials are produced by the neuron.
Depolarization	In biology, depolarization is a change in a cell's membrane potential, making it more positive, or less negative. In neurons and some other cells, a large enough depolarization may result in an action potential. Hyperpolarization is the opposite of depolarization, and inhibits the rise of an action potential.
Excitatory postsynaptic potential	In neuroscience, an excitatory postsynaptic potential is a temporary depolarization of postsynaptic membrane potential caused by the flow of positively charged ions into the postsynaptic cell as a result of opening of ligand-sensitive channels. They are the opposite of inhibitory postsynaptic potentials (IPSPs), which usually result from the flow of negative ions into the cell or positive ions out of the cell.

Hyperpolarization	Hyperpolarization is a change in a cell's membrane potential that makes it more negative. It is the opposite of a depolarization. It inhibits action potentials by increasing the stimulus required to move the membrane potential to the action potential threshold.
Inhibitory postsynaptic potential	An inhibitory postsynaptic potential is a synaptic potential that decreases the chance that a future action potential will occur in a postsynaptic neuron or α-motoneuron. The opposite of an inhibitory postsynaptic potential is an excitatory postsynaptic potential (EPSP), which is a synaptic action that instead increases the probability of the occurrence of a future action potential. They can take place at all chemical synapses which use the secretion of neurotransmitters to create cell to cell signalling.
Neurotransmitter	Neurotransmitters are endogenous chemicals that transmit signals from a neuron to a target cell across a synapse. Neurotransmitters are packaged into synaptic vesicles clustered beneath the membrane in the axon terminal, on the presynaptic side of a synapse. They are released into and diffuse across the synaptic cleft, where they bind to specific receptors in the membrane on the postsynaptic side of the synapse.
Action potential	In physiology, an action potential is a short-lasting event in which the electrical membrane potential of a cell rapidly rises and falls, following a consistent trajectory. Action potentials occur in several types of animal cells, called excitable cells, which include neurons, muscle cells, and endocrine cells, as well as in some plant cells. In neurons, they play a central role in cell-to-cell communication.
Axon hillock	The axon hillock is a specialized part of the cell body (or soma) of a neuron that connects to the axon. As a result, the axon hillock is the last site in the soma where membrane potentials propagated from synaptic inputs are summated before being transmitted to the axon. For many years, it had been believed that the axon hillock was the usual site of action potential initiation.
Refractory period	In physiology, a refractory period is a period of time during which an organ or cell is incapable of repeating a particular action, or (more precisely) the amount of time it takes for an excitable membrane to be ready for a second stimulus once it returns to its resting state following an excitation. It most commonly refers to electrically excitable muscle cells or neurons. After initiation of an action potential, the refractory period is defined two ways:•The absolute refractory period is the interval during which a second action potential absolutely cannot be initiated, no matter how large a stimulus is applied.•The relative refractory period is the interval immediately following during which initiation of a second action potential is inhibited but not impossible. The absolute refractory period coincides with nearly the entire duration of the action potential.

Chapter 4. Neural Conduction and Synaptic Transmission

Interneuron	An interneuron is a neuron that forms a connection between other neurons. Interneurons are neither motor nor sensory. The term is also applied to brain and spinal cord neurons whose axons connect only with nearby neurons, to distinguish them from 'projection' neurons, whose axons (projection fibers) project to more distant regions of the brain or spinal cord.
Myelin	Myelin is a dielectric material that forms a layer, the myelin sheath, usually around only the axon of a neuron. It is essential for the proper functioning of the nervous system. Myelin is an outgrowth of a type of glial cell.
Saltatory conduction	Saltatory conduction is the propagation of action potentials along myelinated axons from one node of Ranvier to the next node, increasing the conduction velocity of action potentials without needing to increase the diameter of an axon. Mechanism Because the cytoplasm of the axon is electrically conductive, and because the myelin inhibits charge leakage through the membrane, depolarization at one node of Ranvier is sufficient to elevate the voltage at a neighboring node. Thus, the voltage at the first node of Ranvier extends spatially to the next node of Ranvier.
Compartmentalization	Compartmentalization is an unconscious psychological defense mechanism used to avoid cognitive dissonance, or the mental discomfort and anxiety caused by a person having conflicting values, cognitions, emotions, beliefs, etc. within themselves. Compartmentalization allows these conflicting ideas to co-exist by inhibiting direct or explicit acknowledgement and interaction between separate compartmentalized self states.
Dendritic spine	A dendritic spine is a small membranous protrusion from a neuron's dendrite that typically receives input from a single synapse of an axon. Dendritic spines serve as a storage site for synaptic strength and help transmit electrical signals to the neuron's cell body. Most spines have a bulbous head (the spine head), and a thin neck that connects the head of the spine to the shaft of the dendrite.
Neurotransmission	Neurotransmission, is the process by which signaling molecules called neurotransmitters are released by a neuron (the presynaptic neuron), and bind to and activate the receptors of another neuron (the postsynaptic neuron). Neurotransmission usually takes place at a synapse, and occurs when an action potential is initiated in the presynaptic neuron. The binding of neurotransmitters to receptors in the postsynaptic neuron can trigger either short term changes, like changes in the membrane potential called postsynaptic potentials, or longer term changes by the activation of signaling cascades.
Microtubule	Microtubules are one of the active matter components of the cytoskeleton. They have a diameter of 25 nm and length varying from 200 nanometers to 25 micrometers.

Ligand	In coordination chemistry, a ligand is an ion or molecule that binds to a central metal atom to form a coordination complex. The bonding between metal and ligand generally involves formal donation of one or more of the ligand's electron pairs. The nature of metal-ligand bonding can range from covalent to ionic. Furthermore, the metal-ligand bond order can range from one to three. Ligands are viewed as Lewis bases, although rare cases are known involving Lewis acidic 'ligands.'
Receptor	In the field of biochemistry, a receptor is a molecule usually found on the surface of a cell, which receives chemical signals from outside the cell. When such external substances attach to a receptor, called 'binding,' they direct a cell to do something. For example to divide, die, or to allow specific substances to enter or exit the cell.
Autoreceptor	An autoreceptor is a receptor located on presynaptic nerve cell membranes and serves as a part of a feedback loop in signal transduction. It is sensitive only to those neurotransmitters or hormones that are released by the neuron in whose membrane the autoreceptor sits. Canonically, a presynaptic neuron releases the neurotransmitter across a synaptic cleft to be detected by the receptors on a postsynaptic neuron.
G protein	G proteins, also known as guanine nucleotide-binding proteins, are a family of proteins involved in transmitting chemical signals originating from outside a cell into the inside of the cell. G proteins function as molecular switches. Their activity is regulated by factors that control their ability to bind to and hydrolyze guanosine triphosphate (GTP) to guanosine diphosphate (GDP).
Metabotropic receptor	Metabotropic receptor is a subtype of membrane receptors at the surface or in vesicles of eukaryotic cells. In the nervous system, based on their structural and functional characteristics, neurotransmitter receptors can be classified into two broad categories: metabotropic and ionotropic receptors. In contrast to the latter, metabotropic receptors do not form an ion channel pore; rather, they are indirectly linked with ion-channels on the plasma membrane of the cell through signal transduction mechanisms, often G proteins.
Second messenger	Second messengers are molecules that relay signals from receptors on the cell surface to target molecules inside the cell, in the cytoplasm or nucleus. They relay the signals of hormones like epinephrine (adrenaline), growth factors, and others, and cause some kind of change in the activity of the cell. They greatly amplify the strength of the signal.
Reuptake	Reuptake, is the reabsorption of a neurotransmitter by a neurotransmitter transporter of a pre-synaptic neuron after it has performed its function of transmitting a neural impulse.

	Reuptake is necessary for normal synaptic physiology because it allows for the recycling of neurotransmitters and regulates the level of neurotransmitter present in the synapse and controls how long a signal resulting from neurotransmitter release lasts. Because neurotransmitters are too large and hydrophilic to diffuse through the membrane, specific transport proteins are necessary for the reabsorption of neurotransmitters.
Acetylcholine	The chemical compound acetylcholine is a neurotransmitter in both the peripheral nervous system (PNS) and central nervous system (CNS) in many organisms including humans. Acetylcholine is one of many neurotransmitters in the autonomic nervous system (ANS) and the only neurotransmitter used in the motor division of the somatic nervous system. (Sensory neurons use glutamate and various peptides at their synapses). Acetylcholine is also the principal neurotransmitter in all autonomic ganglia.
Acetylcholinesterase	Acetylcholinesterase is a serine protease that hydrolyzes the neurotransmitter acetylcholine. AChE is found at mainly neuromuscular junctions and cholinergic brain synapses, where its activity serves to terminate synaptic transmission. It belongs to carboxylesterase family of enzymes.
Astrocyte	Astrocytes (etymology: astron gk. star, cyte gk. cell), also known collectively as astroglia, are characteristic star-shaped glial cells in the brain and spinal cord.
Electrical synapse	An electrical synapse is a mechanical and electrically conductive link between two abutting neurons that is formed at a narrow gap between the pre- and postsynaptic neurons known as a gap junction. At gap junctions, such cells approach within about 3.5 nm of each other, a much shorter distance than the 20 to 40 nm distance that separates cells at chemical synapse. In organisms, electrical synapse-based systems co-exist with chemical synapses.
Carbon monoxide	Carbon monoxide is a colorless, odorless and tasteless gas which is slightly lighter than air. It is highly toxic to humans and animals in higher quantities, although it is also produced in normal animal metabolism in low quantities, and is thought to have some normal biological functions. It consists of one carbon atom and one oxygen atom, connected by a triple bond which consists of two covalent bonds as well as one dative covalent bond. It is the simplest oxocarbon. In coordination complexes the carbon monoxide ligand is called carbonyl.
Catecholamine	Catecholamines are 'fight-or-flight' hormones released by the adrenal glands in response to stress. They are part of the sympathetic nervous system. They are called catecholamines because they contain a catechol or 3,4-dihydroxylphenyl group.

Dopamine	Dopamine, a simple organic chemical in the catecholamine family, plays a number of important physiological roles in the bodies of animals. Its name derives from its chemical structure, which consists of an amine group (NH_2) linked to a catechol structure called dihydroxyphenethylamine, the decarboxyalted form of dihydroxyphenylalanine (acronym DOPA). In the brain, dopamine functions as a neurotransmitter--a chemical released by nerve cells to send signals to other nerve cells.
Epinephrine	Epinephrine is a hormone and a neurotransmitter. Epinephrine has many functions in the body, regulating heart rate, blood vessel and air passage diameters, and metabolic shifts; epinephrine release is a crucial component of the fight-or-flight response of the sympathetic nervous system. In chemical terms, epinephrine is one of a group of monoamines called the catecholamines.
Indolamines	Indolamines are a family of neurotransmitters that share a common molecular structure (namely, indolamine). A common example of an indolamine is serotonin,a neurotransmitter involved in mood and sleep. Another example of an indolamine is melatonin, which regulates the sleep-wake cycle (circadian rhythm) in humans.
Norepinephrine	Norepinephrine , or noradrenaline (BAN) , is a catecholamine with multiple roles including as a hormone and a neurotransmitter. Areas of the body that produce or are affected by norepinephrine are described as noradrenergic. The terms noradrenaline and norepinephrine are interchangeable, with noradrenaline being the common name in most parts of the world.
Serotonin	Serotonin is a monoamine neurotransmitter. Biochemically derived from tryptophan, serotonin is primarily found in the gastrointestinal (GI) tract, platelets, and in the central nervous system (CNS) of animals including humans. It is a well-known contributor to feelings of well-being; therefore it is also known as a 'happiness hormone' despite not being a hormone.
Tyrosine	Tyrosine or 4-hydroxyphenylalanine, is one of the 22 amino acids that are used by cells to synthesize proteins. Its codons are UAC and UAU. It is a non-essential amino acid with a polar side group. The word 'tyrosine' is from the Greek tyri, meaning cheese, as it was first discovered in 1846 by German chemist Justus von Liebig in the protein casein from cheese.
Endorphin	Endorphins ('endogenous morphine') are endogenous opioid peptides that function as neurotransmitters. They are produced by the pituitary gland and the hypothalamus in vertebrates during exercise, excitement, pain, consumption of spicy food, love and orgasm, and they resemble the opiates in their abilities to produce analgesia and a feeling of well-being.

Chapter 4. Neural Conduction and Synaptic Transmission

Neuropeptide	Neuropeptides are small protein-like molecules used by neurons to communicate with each other, distinct from the larger neurotransmitters. They are neuronal signaling molecules, influence the activity of the brain in specific ways and are thus involved in particular brain functions, like analgesia, reward, food intake, learning and memory. Neuropeptides are expressed and released by neurons, and mediate or modulate neuronal communication by acting on cell surface receptors.
Agonist	An agonist is a chemical that binds to a receptor of a cell and triggers a response by that cell. Agonists often mimic the action of a naturally occurring substance. Whereas an agonist causes an action, an antagonist blocks the action of the agonist and an inverse agonist causes an action opposite to that of the agonist.
Cocaine	Cocaine benzoylmethylecgonine (INN) is a crystalline tropane alkaloid that is obtained from the leaves of the coca plant. The name comes from 'coca' in addition to the alkaloid suffix -ine, forming cocaine. It is a stimulant of the central nervous system, an appetite suppressant, and a topical anesthetic. Specifically, it is a serotonin-norepinephrine-dopamine reuptake inhibitor, which mediates functionality of these neurotransmitters as an exogenous catecholamine transporter ligand. Because of the way it affects the mesolimbic reward pathway, cocaine is addictive.
Synaptic vesicle	In a neuron, synaptic vesicles store various neurotransmitters that are released at the synapse. The release is regulated by a voltage-dependent calcium channel. Vesicles are essential for propagating nerve impulses between neurons and are constantly recreated by the cell.
Psychoactive drug	A psychoactive drug, psychopharmaceutical, or psychotropic is a chemical substance that crosses the blood-brain barrier and acts primarily upon the central nervous system where it affects brain function, resulting in changes in perception, mood, consciousness, cognition, and behavior. These substances may be used recreationally, to purposefully alter one's consciousness, as entheogens, for ritual, spiritual, and/or shamanic purposes, as a tool for studying or augmenting the mind, or therapeutically as medication. Because psychoactive substances bring about subjective changes in consciousness and mood that the user may find pleasant (e.g. euphoria) or advantageous (e.g. increased alertness), many psychoactive substances are abused, that is, used excessively, despite the health risks or negative consequences.
Anticonvulsant	The anticonvulsants (also commonly known as antiepileptic drugs) are a diverse group of pharmaceuticals used in the treatment of epileptic seizures. Anticonvulsants are also increasingly being used in the treatment of bipolar disorder, since many seem to act as mood stabilizers, and for the treatment of neuropathic pain.

Anxiolytic	An anxiolytic is a drug used for the treatment of anxiety and its related psychological and physical symptoms. Anxiolytics have been shown to be useful in the treatment of anxiety disorders. Beta-receptor blockers such as propranolol and oxprenolol, although not anxiolytics, can be used to combat the somatic symptoms of anxiety.
Benzodiazepine	A benzodiazepine is a psychoactive drug whose core chemical structure is the fusion of a benzene ring and a diazepine ring. The first benzodiazepine, chlordiazepoxide (Librium), was discovered accidentally by Leo Sternbach in 1955, and made available in 1960 by Hoffmann-La Roche, which has also marketed diazepam (Valium) since 1963. Benzodiazepines enhance the effect of the neurotransmitter gamma-aminobutyric acid (GABA), which results in sedative, hypnotic (sleep-inducing), anxiolytic (anti-anxiety), anticonvulsant, muscle relaxant and amnesic action.
Chlordiazepoxide	Chlordiazepoxide is a sedativehypnotic drug and benzodiazepine. It is marketed under the trade names Angirex, Elenium, Klopoxid, Librax (also contains clidinium bromide), Libritabs, Librium, Mesural, Multum, Novapam, Risolid, Silibrin, Sonimen and Tropium. Chlordiazepoxide was the first benzodiazepine to be synthesised and the discovery of chlordiazepoxide was by pure chance.
Diazepam	Diazepam first marketed as Valium by Hoffmann-La Roche, is a benzodiazepine drug. Diazepam is also marketed in Australia as Antenex. It is commonly used for treating anxiety, insomnia, seizures including status epilepticus, muscle spasms (such as in cases of tetanus), restless legs syndrome, alcohol withdrawal, benzodiazepine withdrawal and Ménière's disease.
Sedative	A sedative is a substance that induces sedation by reducing irritability or excitement. At higher doses it may result in slurred speech, staggering gait, poor judgment, and slow, uncertain reflexes. Doses of sedatives such as benzodiazepines, when used as a hypnotic to induce sleep, tend to be higher than amounts used to relieve anxiety, whereas only low doses are needed to provide a peaceful and calming sedative effect.

Chapter 4. Neural Conduction and Synaptic Transmission

1. _____ is a serine protease that hydrolyzes the neurotransmitter acetylcholine. AChE is found at mainly neuromuscular junctions and cholinergic brain synapses, where its activity serves to terminate synaptic transmission. It belongs to carboxylesterase family of enzymes.

   a. apnea
   b. Acetylcholinesterase
   c. Vasopressin
   d. 2-Arachidonoylglycerol

2. The _____s (also commonly known as antiepileptic drugs) are a diverse group of pharmaceuticals used in the treatment of epileptic seizures. _____s are also increasingly being used in the treatment of bipolar disorder, since many seem to act as mood stabilizers, and for the treatment of neuropathic pain. The goal of an _____ is to suppress the rapid and excessive firing of neurons that start a seizure.

   a. Anticonvulsant
   b. Epilepsy Foundation of Victoria
   c. Epilepsy PhenomeGenome Project
   d. Ictal asystole

3. In biology, _____ is a change in a cell's membrane potential, making it more positive, or less negative. In neurons and some other cells, a large enough _____ may result in an action potential. Hyperpolarization is the opposite of _____, and inhibits the rise of an action potential.

   a. Diagonal band of Broca
   b. Diffuse neuro-endocrine system
   c. Digastric branch of facial nerve
   d. Depolarization

4. _____ or 4-hydroxyphenylalanine, is one of the 22 amino acids that are used by cells to synthesize proteins. Its codons are UAC and UAU. It is a non-essential amino acid with a polar side group. The word '_____' is from the Greek tyri, meaning cheese, as it was first discovered in 1846 by German chemist Justus von Liebig in the protein casein from cheese.

   a. Tyrosine phosphorylation
   b. Valine
   c. Carl Rogers theory evaluation
   d. Tyrosine

5. . _____s are the branched projections of a neuron that act to conduct the electrochemical stimulation received from other neural cells to the cell body, or soma, of the neuron from which the _____s project. Electrical stimulation is transmitted onto _____s by upstream neurons via synapses which are located at various points throughout the dendritic arbor. _____s play a critical role in integrating these synaptic inputs and in determining the extent to which action potentials are produced by the neuron.

a. Dendrite

b. Carl Rogers theory evaluation

c. massed learning

d. Sacral ganglia

1. b
2. a
3. d
4. d
5. a

You can take the complete Chapter Practice Test

for Chapter 4. Neural Conduction and Synaptic Transmission
on all key terms, persons, places, and concepts.

Online 99 Cents

http://www.epub3.10.9241.4.cram101.com/

Use www.Cram101.com for all your study needs

including Cram101's online interactive problem solving labs in

chemistry, statistics, mathematics, and more.

	Brain tumor
	Neuroimaging
	Cerebral angiography
	X-ray computed tomography
	Magnetic resonance imaging
	Positron emission tomography
	Color agnosia
	Functional MRI
	Electroencephalography
	Magnetoencephalography
	Transcranial magnetic stimulation
	Event-related potential
	Electromyography
	Electrooculography
	Hypertension
	Amygdala
	Dopamine
	Injection
	Norepinephrine

_____ | Antibody

_____ | Ligand

_____ | Messenger RNA

_____ | Neurologist

_____ | Digit Span

_____ | Intelligence quotient

_____ | Wechsler Adult Intelligence Scale

_____ | Dichotic listening test

_____ | Episodic memory

_____ | Explicit memory

_____ | Implicit memory

_____ | Semantic memory

_____ | Cerebral cortex

_____ | Cognition

_____ | Dyslexia

_____ | Perseveration

_____ | Phonology

_____ | Semantics

_____ | Wisconsin Card Sorting Test

	Anxiolytic
	Elevated plus maze
	Sexual intercourse
	Paradigm
	Conditioned taste aversion
	Pleasure center
	Taste aversion
	Spatial memory
	Anxiety

| Brain tumor | A brain tumor is an intracranial solid neoplasm, a tumor (defined as an abnormal growth of cells) within the brain or the central spinal canal.

Brain tumors include all tumors inside the cranium or in the central spinal canal. They are created by an abnormal and uncontrolled cell division, normally either in the brain itself (neurons, glial cells (astrocytes, oligodendrocytes, ependymal cells, myelin-producing Schwann cells), lymphatic tissue, blood vessels), in the cranial nerves, in the brain envelopes (meninges), skull, pituitary and pineal gland, or spread from cancers primarily located in other organs (metastatic tumors). |
| --- | --- |
| Neuroimaging | Neuroimaging includes the use of various techniques to either directly or indirectly image the structure, function/pharmacology of the brain. It is a relatively new discipline within medicine and neuroscience/psychology. |

Chapter 5. The Research Methods of Biopsychology

CHAPTER HIGHLIGHTS & NOTES: KEY TERMS, PEOPLE, PLACES, CONCEPTS

Cerebral angiography	Cerebral angiography is a form of angiography which provides images of blood vessels in and around the brain, thereby allowing detection of abnormalities such as arteriovenous malformations and aneurysms. It was pioneered in 1927 by the Portuguese physician Egas Moniz at the University of Lisbon, who also helped develop thorotrast for use in the procedure. Typically a catheter is inserted into a large artery (such as the femoral artery) and threaded through the circulatory system to the carotid artery, where a contrast agent is injected.
X-ray computed tomography	X-ray computed tomography is a medical imaging method employing tomography created by computer processing. Digital geometry processing is used to generate a three-dimensional image of the inside of an object from a large series of two-dimensional X-ray images taken around a single axis of rotation. X-ray computed tomography produces a volume of data which can be manipulated, through a process known as 'windowing', in order to demonstrate various bodily structures based on their ability to block the X-ray beam.
Magnetic resonance imaging	Magnetic resonance imaging nuclear magnetic resonance imaging or magnetic resonance tomography (MRT) is a medical imaging technique used in radiology to visualize internal structures of the body in detail. Magnetic resonance imaging makes use of the property of nuclear magnetic resonance (NMR) to image nuclei of atoms inside the body. An Magnetic resonance imaging scanner is a device in which the patient lies within a large, powerful magnet where the magnetic field is used to align the magnetization of some atomic nuclei in the body, and radio frequency magnetic fields are applied to systematically alter the alignment of this magnetization.
Positron emission tomography	Positron emission tomography is a nuclear medicine imaging technique that produces a three-dimensional image or picture of functional processes in the body. The system detects pairs of gamma rays emitted indirectly by a positron-emitting radionuclide (tracer), which is introduced into the body on a biologically active molecule. Three-dimensional images of tracer concentration within the body are then constructed by computer analysis.
Color agnosia	Color agnosia, is a medical or psychological condition that prevents a person from correctly associating hue names with common objects. The sufferer retains the ability of distinguishing hues. It is a specific form of agnosia and generally results from damage to the visual cortex, often in V4 (as opposed to most other kinds of color blindness, which stem from problems with the photoreceptor cells).
Functional MRI	Functional MRI is a type of specialized MRI scan.

	It measures the hemodynamic response (change in blood flow) related to neural activity in the brain or spinal cord of humans or other animals. It is one of the most recently developed forms of neuroimaging. Since the early 1990s, Functional MRI has come to dominate the brain mapping field due to its relatively low invasiveness, absence of radiation exposure, and relatively wide availability.
Electroencephalography	Electroencephalography is the recording of electrical activity along the scalp. EEG measures voltage fluctuations resulting from ionic current flows within the neurons of the brain. In clinical contexts, EEG refers to the recording of the brain's spontaneous electrical activity over a short period of time, usually 20-40 minutes, as recorded from multiple electrodes placed on the scalp.
Magnetoencephalography	Magnetoencephalography is a technique for mapping brain activity by recording magnetic fields produced by electrical currents occurring naturally in the brain, using arrays of SQUIDs (superconducting quantum interference devices). Applications of MEG include basic research into perceptual and cognitive brain processes, localizing regions affected by pathology before surgical removal, determining the function of various parts of the brain, and neurofeedback. History of MEG MEG signals were first measured by University of Illinois physicist David Cohen in 1968, before the availability of the SQUID, using a copper induction coil as the detector.
Transcranial magnetic stimulation	Transcranial magnetic stimulation is a noninvasive method to cause depolarization or hyperpolarization in the neurons of the brain. Transcranial magnetic stimulation uses electromagnetic induction to induce weak electric currents using a rapidly changing magnetic field; this can cause activity in specific or general parts of the brain with minimal discomfort, allowing the functioning and interconnections of the brain to be studied. A variant of Transcranial magnetic stimulation, repetitive transcranial magnetic stimulation has been tested as a treatment tool for various neurological and psychiatric disorders including migraines, strokes, Parkinson's disease, dystonia, tinnitus, depression and auditory hallucinations.
Event-related potential	An event-related potential is any measured brain response that is directly the result of a thought or perception. More formally, it is any stereotyped electrophysiological response to an internal or external stimulus. Event-related potentials are measured with electroencephalography (EEG).
Electromyography	Electromyography is a technique for evaluating and recording the electrical activity produced by skeletal muscles. EMG is performed using an instrument called an electromyograph, to produce a record called an electromyogram. An electromyograph detects the electrical potential generated by muscle cells when these cells are electrically or neurologically activated.
Electrooculography	Electrooculography. is a technique for measuring the resting potential of the retina.

Chapter 5. The Research Methods of Biopsychology

Hypertension	Hypertension or high blood pressure, sometimes called arterial hypertension, is a chronic medical condition in which the blood pressure in the arteries is elevated. This requires the heart to work harder than normal to circulate blood through the blood vessels. Blood pressure is summarised by two measurements, systolic and diastolic, which depend on whether the heart muscle is contracting (systole) or relaxed between beats (diastole).
Amygdala	The are almond-shaped groups of nuclei located deep within the medial temporal lobes of the brain in complex vertebrates, including humans. Shown in research to perform a primary role in the processing of memory and emotional reactions, the amygdalae are considered part of the limbic system. Anatomical subdivisions
	The regions described as amygdala nuclei encompass several structures with distinct connectional and functional characteristics in animals and humans.
Dopamine	Dopamine, a simple organic chemical in the catecholamine family, plays a number of important physiological roles in the bodies of animals. Its name derives from its chemical structure, which consists of an amine group (NH_2) linked to a catechol structure called dihydroxyphenethylamine, the decarboxyalted form of dihydroxyphenylalanine (acronym DOPA). In the brain, dopamine functions as a neurotransmitter--a chemical released by nerve cells to send signals to other nerve cells.
Injection	An injection (often referred to as a 'shot' or a 'jab') is an infusion method of putting fluid into the body, usually with a hollow needle and a syringe which is pierced through the skin to a sufficient depth for the material to be forced into the body. An injection follows a parenteral route of administration; that is, administered other than through the digestive tract.
	There are several methods of injection or infusion, including intradermal, subcutaneous, intramuscular, intravenous, intraosseous, and intraperitoneal.
Norepinephrine	Norepinephrine , or noradrenaline (BAN) , is a catecholamine with multiple roles including as a hormone and a neurotransmitter. Areas of the body that produce or are affected by norepinephrine are described as noradrenergic.
	The terms noradrenaline and norepinephrine are interchangeable, with noradrenaline being the common name in most parts of the world.
Antibody	An antibody is a large Y-shaped protein used by the immune system to identify and neutralize foreign objects like bacteria and viruses. The antibody recognizes a unique part of the foreign target, termed an antigen. Each tip of the 'Y' of an antibody contains a paratope (a structure analogous to a lock) that is specific for one particular epitope (that is equivelent to a key) on an antigen, allowing these two structures to bind together with precision.

	Using this binding mechanism, an antibody can tag a microbe or an infected cell for attack by other parts of the immune system, or can neutralize its target directly (for example, by blocking a part of a microbe that is essential for its invasion and survival). The production of antibodies is the main function of the humoral immune system.
Ligand	In coordination chemistry, a ligand is an ion or molecule that binds to a central metal atom to form a coordination complex. The bonding between metal and ligand generally involves formal donation of one or more of the ligand's electron pairs. The nature of metal-ligand bonding can range from covalent to ionic. Furthermore, the metal-ligand bond order can range from one to three. Ligands are viewed as Lewis bases, although rare cases are known involving Lewis acidic 'ligands.'
Messenger RNA	Messenger RNA is a molecule of RNA encoding a chemical 'blueprint' for a protein product. mRNA is transcribed from a DNA template, and carries coding information to the sites of protein synthesis: the ribosomes. Here, the nucleic acid polymer is translated into a polymer of amino acids: a protein.
Neurologist	A neurologist is a physician who specializes in neurology, and is trained to investigate, or diagnose and treat neurological disorders.

Neurology is the medical specialty related to the human nervous system. The nervous system encompasses the brain, spinal cord, and peripheral nerves. |
Digit Span	In psychology and neuroscience, memory span is the longest list of items that a person can repeat back in correct order immediately after presentation on 50% of all trials. Items may include words, numbers, or letters. The task is known as digit span when numbers are used.
Intelligence quotient	An intelligence quotient, is a score derived from one of several standardized tests designed to assess intelligence. The abbreviation 'IQ' comes from the German term Intelligenz-Quotient, originally coined by psychologist William Stern. When modern IQ tests are devised, the mean (average) score within an age group is set to 100 and the standard deviation (SD) almost always to 15, although this was not always so historically.
Wechsler Adult Intelligence Scale	The Wechsler Adult Intelligence Scale is a test designed to measure intelligence in adults and older adolescents. It is currently in its fourth edition (WAIS-IV). The original WAIS (Form I) was published in February 1955 by David Wechsler, as a revision of the Wechsler-Bellevue Intelligence Scale.
Dichotic listening test	In cognitive psychology and neuroscience, dichotic listening is a procedure commonly used to investigate selective attention in the auditory system.

	More specifically, it is 'used as a behavioral test for hemispheric lateralization of speech sound perception.' During a standard dichotic listening test, a participant is simultaneously presented with two different auditory stimuli (usually speech) separately to each ear over headphones. Participants are asked to distinguish/identify one or (in a divided-attention experiment) both of the stimuli.
Episodic memory	Episodic memory is the memory of autobiographical events (times, places, associated emotions, and other contextual knowledge) that can be explicitly stated. Semantic and episodic memory together make up the category of declarative memory, which is one of the two major divisions in memory. The counterpart to declarative, or explicit memory, is procedural memory, or implicit memory.
Explicit memory	Explicit memory is the conscious, intentional recollection of previous experiences and information. People use explicit memory throughout the day, such as remembering the time of an appointment or recollecting an event from years ago. Explicit memory involves conscious recollection, compared with implicit memory which is an unconscious, nonintentional form of memory.
Implicit memory	Implicit memory is a type of memory in which previous experiences aid in the performance of a task without conscious awareness of these previous experiences. Evidence for implicit memory arises in priming, a process whereby subjects are measured by how they have improved their performance on tasks for which they have been subconsciously prepared. Implicit memory also leads to the illusion-of-truth effect, which suggests that subjects are more likely to rate as true those statements that they have already heard, regardless of their veracity.
Semantic memory	Semantic memory refers to the memory of meanings, understandings, and other concept-based knowledge unrelated to specific experiences. The conscious recollection of factual information and general knowledge about the world is generally thought to be independent of context and personal relevance. Semantic and episodic memory together make up the category of declarative memory, which is one of the two major divisions in memory.
Cerebral cortex	The cerebral cortex is a sheet of neural tissue that is outermost to the cerebrum of the mammalian brain. It plays a key role in memory, attention, perceptual awareness, thought, language, and consciousness. It is constituted of up to six horizontal layers, each of which has a different composition in terms of neurons and connectivity.
Cognition	In science, cognition is a group of mental processes that includes attention, memory, producing and understanding language, solving problems, and making decisions. Cognition is studied in various disciplines such as psychology, philosophy, linguistics, science and computer science.

Dyslexia	Dyslexia is a very broad term defining a learning disability that impairs a person's fluency or comprehension accuracy in being able to read, and which can manifest itself as a difficulty with phonological awareness, phonological decoding, orthographic coding, auditory short-term memory, or rapid naming. Dyslexia is distinct from reading difficulties resulting from other causes, such as a non-neurological deficiency with vision or hearing, or from poor or inadequate reading instruction. It is believed that dyslexia can affect between 5 and 10 percent of a given population although there have been no studies to indicate an accurate percentage.
Perseveration	Perseveration is the repetition of a particular response, such as a word, phrase, or gesture, despite the absence or cessation of a stimulus, usually caused by brain injury or other organic disorder. If an issue has been fully explored and discussed to a point of resolution, it is not uncommon for something to trigger the re-investigation of the matter. This can happen at any time during a conversation. This is particularly true with those who have had traumatic brain injuries.
Phonology	Phonology is a British peer-reviewed journal of phonology published by Cambridge University Press, the only journal devoted exclusively to this subfield of linguistics. The current editors are Prof. Colin J. Ewen (Leiden University) and Prof.
Semantics	Semantics is the study of meaning. It focuses on the relation between signifiers, such as words, phrases, signs, and symbols, and what they stand for, their denotata. Linguistic semantics is the study of meaning that is used to understand human expression through language.
Wisconsin Card Sorting Test	The Wisconsin Card Sorting Test (WCST) is a neuropsychological test of 'set-shifting', i.e. the ability to display flexibility in the face of changing schedules of reinforcement. The Wisconsin Card Sorting Test was written by David A. Grant and Esta A. Berg. Initially, a number of stimulus cards are presented to the participant. The shapes on the cards are different in color, quantity, and design. The person administering the test decides whether the cards are to be matched by color, design or quantity. The participant is then given a stack of additional cards and asked to match each one to one of the stimulus cards, thereby forming separate piles of cards for each. The participant is not told how to match the cards; however, he or she is told whether a particular match is right or wrong. During the course of the test the matching rules are changed and the time taken for the participant to learn the new rules, and the mistakes made during this learning process are analysed to arrive at a score.

Chapter 5. The Research Methods of Biopsychology

Anxiolytic	An anxiolytic is a drug used for the treatment of anxiety and its related psychological and physical symptoms. Anxiolytics have been shown to be useful in the treatment of anxiety disorders. Beta-receptor blockers such as propranolol and oxprenolol, although not anxiolytics, can be used to combat the somatic symptoms of anxiety.
Elevated plus maze	The elevated plus maze is a rodent model of anxiety that is used as a screening test for putative anxiolytic or anxiogenic compounds and as a general research tool in neurobiological anxiety research. The test setting consists of a plus-shaped apparatus with two open and two enclosed arms, each with an open roof, elevated 40-70 cm from the floor. The model is based on rodents' aversion of open spaces.
Sexual intercourse	Sexual intercourse, commonly refers to the act in which the male reproductive organ enters the female reproductive tract. The two entities may be of opposite sexes, or they may be hermaphroditic, as is the case with snails. The definition may additionally include penetrative sexual acts between same-sex pairings, such as penetration of non-sexual organs (oral intercourse, anal intercourse) or by non-sexual organs (fingering, tonguing), which are also commonly practiced by heterosexual couples.
Paradigm	In the behavioural sciences, e.g. Psychology, Biology, Neurosciences, an experimental paradigm is an experimental setup (i.e. a way to conduct a certain type of experiment) that is defined by certain fine-tuned standards and often has a theoretical background. A paradigm in this technical sense, however, is not a way of thinking as it is in the epistemological meaning. See also: Paradigm, Design of experiments
Conditioned taste aversion	Conditioned taste aversion, a term coined by Seligman and Hager, is an example of classical conditioning or Pavlovian conditioning. Conditioned taste aversion occurs when a subject associates the taste of a certain food with symptoms caused by a toxic, spoiled, or poisonous substance. Generally, taste aversion is caused after ingestion of the food causes nausea, sickness, or vomiting. The ability to develop a taste aversion is considered an adaptive trait or survival mechanism that trains the body to avoid poisonous substances (e.g., poisonous berries) before they can cause harm.
Pleasure center	Pleasure center is the general term used for the brain regions involved in pleasure. Discoveries made in the 1950s initially suggested that rodents could not stop electrically stimulating parts of their brain, mainly the nucleus accumbens, which was theorized to produce great pleasure.

Taste aversion	Conditioned taste aversion, also known as Garcia effect (after Dr. John Garcia), and as 'Sauce-Bearnaise Syndrome', a term coined by Seligman and Hager, is an example of classical conditioning or Pavlovian conditioning. Conditioned taste aversion occurs when a subject associates the taste of a certain food with symptoms caused by a toxic, spoiled, or poisonous substance. Generally, taste aversion is caused after ingestion of the food causes nausea, sickness, or vomiting.
Spatial memory	In cognitive psychology and neuroscience, spatial memory is the part of memory responsible for recording information about one's environment and its spatial orientation. For example, a person's spatial memory is required in order to navigate around a familiar city, just as a rat's spatial memory is needed to learn the location of food at the end of a maze. It is often argued that a person's or animal's spatial memories are summarised in a cognitive map.
Anxiety	Anxiety is a psychological and physiological state characterized by somatic, emotional, cognitive, and behavioral components. The root meaning of the word anxiety is 'to vex or trouble'; in either the absence or presence of psychological stress, anxiety can create feelings of fear, worry, uneasiness and dread. Anxiety is considered to be a normal reaction to stress.

1. A _____ is a physician who specializes in neurology, and is trained to investigate, or diagnose and treat neurological disorders.

    Neurology is the medical specialty related to the human nervous system. The nervous system encompasses the brain, spinal cord, and peripheral nerves.

    a. Neuromuscular diagnostic
    b. Neuronal tuning
    c. Neurologist
    d. Neuroplasticity

2. . _____, is a medical or psychological condition that prevents a person from correctly associating hue names with common objects. The sufferer retains the ability of distinguishing hues. It is a specific form of agnosia and generally results from damage to the visual cortex, often in V4 (as opposed to most other kinds of color blindness, which stem from problems with the photoreceptor cells).

    a. Comparative neuropsychology
    b. Color agnosia
    c. Cultural neuroscience

Visit Cram101.com for full Practice Exams

Chapter 5. The Research Methods of Biopsychology

3. _____, a term coined by Seligman and Hager, is an example of classical conditioning or Pavlovian conditioning. _____ occurs when a subject associates the taste of a certain food with symptoms caused by a toxic, spoiled, or poisonous substance. Generally, taste aversion is caused after ingestion of the food causes nausea, sickness, or vomiting. The ability to develop a taste aversion is considered an adaptive trait or survival mechanism that trains the body to avoid poisonous substances (e.g., poisonous berries) before they can cause harm.

   a. Monell Chemical Senses Center
   b. Taste receptor
   c. Tastes like chicken
   d. Conditioned taste aversion

4. _____ is a very broad term defining a learning disability that impairs a person's fluency or comprehension accuracy in being able to read, and which can manifest itself as a difficulty with phonological awareness, phonological decoding, orthographic coding, auditory short-term memory, or rapid naming.

   _____ is distinct from reading difficulties resulting from other causes, such as a non-neurological deficiency with vision or hearing, or from poor or inadequate reading instruction. It is believed that _____ can affect between 5 and 10 percent of a given population although there have been no studies to indicate an accurate percentage.

   a. Dyslexia
   b. Formative assessment
   c. Generation effect
   d. Goal theory

5. A _____ is an intracranial solid neoplasm, a tumor (defined as an abnormal growth of cells) within the brain or the central spinal canal.

   _____s include all tumors inside the cranium or in the central spinal canal. They are created by an abnormal and uncontrolled cell division, normally either in the brain itself (neurons, glial cells (astrocytes, oligodendrocytes, ependymal cells, myelin-producing Schwann cells), lymphatic tissue, blood vessels), in the cranial nerves, in the brain envelopes (meninges), skull, pituitary and pineal gland, or spread from cancers primarily located in other organs (metastatic tumors).

   a. Brain tumor
   b. Brain morphometry
   c. Brainstem
   d. Broca's area

1. c
2. b
3. d
4. a
5. a

You can take the complete Chapter Practice Test

for Chapter 5. The Research Methods of Biopsychology
on all key terms, persons, places, and concepts.

Online 99 Cents

http://www.epub3.10.9241.5.cram101.com/

Use www.Cram101.com for all your study needs

including Cram101's online interactive problem solving labs in

chemistry, statistics, mathematics, and more.

Chapter 6. The Visual System

CHAPTER OUTLINE: KEY TERMS, PEOPLE, PLACES, CONCEPTS

	Brightness
	Accommodation
	Amacrine cells
	Binocular disparity
	Bipolar cell
	Convergence
	Lateral communication
	Retina
	Retinal ganglion cell
	Blind spot
	Fovea centralis
	Photopic vision
	Scotopic vision
	Purkinje effect
	Rhodopsin
	Transduction
	Lateral inhibition
	Mach bands
	Complex cell

Chapter 6. The Visual System

_____ Ocular dominance column

_____ Sine

_____ Fourier analysis

_____ Color vision

_____ Complementary color

_____ Color constancy

CHAPTER HIGHLIGHTS & NOTES: KEY TERMS, PEOPLE, PLACES, CONCEPTS

Brightness	Brightness is an attribute of visual perception in which a source appears to be radiating or reflecting light. In other words, brightness is the perception elicited by the luminance of a visual target. This is a subjective attribute/property of an object being observed.
Accommodation	Accommodation (Acc) is the process by which the vertebrate eye changes optical power to maintain a clear image (focus) on an object as its distance varies.
	Accommodation acts like a reflex, but can also be consciously controlled. Mammals, birds and reptiles vary the optical power by changing the form of the elastic lens using the ciliary body (in humans up to 15 diopters).
Amacrine cells	Amacrine cells are interneurons in the retina. Amacrine cells are responsible for 70% of input to retinal ganglion cells. Bipolar cells, which are responsible for the other 30% of input to retinal ganglia, are regulated by amacrine cells.
Binocular disparity	Binocular disparity refers to the difference in image location of an object seen by the left and right eyes, resulting from the eyes' horizontal separation. The brain uses binocular disparity to extract depth information from the two-dimensional retinal images in stereopsis. In computer vision, binocular disparity refers to the difference in coordinates of similar features within two stereo images.

Bipolar cell	A bipolar cell is a type of neuron which has two extensions. Bipolar cells are specialized sensory neurons for the transmission of special senses. As such, they are part of the sensory pathways for smell, sight, taste, hearing and vestibular functions.
Convergence	Precisely every individual in the population is identical. While full convergence might be seen in genetic algorithms using only cross over, such convergence is seldom seen in genetic programming using Koza's subtree swapping crossover. However, populations often stabilise after a time, in the sense that the best programs all have a common ancestor and their behaviour is very similar both to each other and to that of high fitness programs from the previous generations.
Lateral communication	In organizations and organisms, lateral communication works in contrast to traditional top-down, bottom-up or hierarchic communication and involves the spreading of messages from individuals across the base of a pyramid.

Lateral communication in organism or animals can give rise to Collective intelligence, or the appearance of Collective intelligence.

Examples of lateral communication in organisms include:•A coordinated flock of birds or a shoal of fish all maintain their relative positions, or alter direction simultaneously due to lateral communication amongst members; this is achieved due to tiny pressure variations.•An ants, termites, bees nest is not coordinated by messages sent by the queen ant / bee / termite but by the lateral communication, mediated by scent trails of the ants. |
Retina	The vertebrate retina is a light-sensitive tissue lining the inner surface of the eye. The optics of the eye create an image of the visual world on the retina, which serves much the same function as the film in a camera. Light striking the retina initiates a cascade of chemical and electrical events that ultimately trigger nerve impulses.
Retinal ganglion cell	A retinal ganglion cell is a type of neuron located near the inner surface (the ganglion cell layer) of the retina of the eye. It receives visual information from photoreceptors via two intermediate neuron types: bipolar cells and amacrine cells. Retinal ganglion cells collectively transmit image-forming and non-image forming visual information from the retina to several regions in the thalamus, hypothalamus, and mesencephalon, or midbrain.
Blind spot	A blind spot, scotoma, is an obscuration of the visual field. A particular blind spot known as the blindspot, or physiological blind spot, or punctum caecum in medical literature, is the place in the visual field that corresponds to the lack of light-detecting photoreceptor cells on the optic disc of the retina where the optic nerve passes through it. Since there are no cells to detect light on the optic disc, a part of the field of vision is not perceived.

Chapter 6. The Visual System

Fovea centralis	The fovea centralis, also generally known as the fovea, is a part of the eye, located in the center of the macula region of the retina. The fovea is responsible for sharp central vision (also called foveal vision), which is necessary in humans for reading, watching television or movies, driving, and any activity where visual detail is of primary importance. The fovea is surrounded by the parafovea belt, and the perifovea outer region: The parafovea is the intermediate belt, where the ganglion cell layer is composed of more than five rows of cells, as well as the highest density of cones; the perifovea is the outermost region where the ganglion cell layer contains two to four rows of cells, and is where visual acuity is below the optimum.
Photopic vision	Photopic vision is the vision of the eye under well-lit conditions. In humans and many other animals, photopic vision allows color perception, mediated by cone cells, and a significantly higher visual acuity and temporal resolution than available with scotopic vision. The human eye uses three types of cones to sense light in three respective bands of color.
Scotopic vision	Scotopic vision is the vision of the eye under low light conditions. The term comes from Greek skotos meaning darkness and -opia meaning a condition of sight. In the human eye cone cells are nonfunctional in low light - scotopic vision is produced exclusively through rod cells which are most sensitive to wavelengths of light around 498 nm (green-blue) and are insensitive to wavelengths longer than about 640 nm (red).
Purkinje effect	The Purkinje effect (sometimes called the Purkinje shift. This effect introduces a difference in color contrast under different levels of illumination. For instance, in bright sunlight, geranium flowers appear bright red against the dull green of their leaves, or adjacent blue flowers, but in the same scene viewed at dusk, the contrast is reversed, with the red petals appearing a dark red or black, and the leaves and blue petals appearing relatively bright.
Rhodopsin	Rhodopsin, is a biological pigment of the retina that is responsible for both the formation of the photoreceptor cells and the first events in the perception of light. Rhodopsins belong to the G-protein coupled receptor family and are extremely sensitive to light, enabling vision in low-light conditions. Exposed to light, the pigment immediately photobleaches, and it takes about 30 minutes to regenerate fully in humans.
Transduction	Transduction is the transformation of one form of energy to another. In psychology, transduction refers to the nervous system. In the system, transduction occurs when environmental energy is transformed into electrical or neural energy.

Lateral inhibition	In neurobiology, lateral inhibition is the capacity of an excited neuron to reduce the activity of its neighbors. Lateral inhibition sharpens the spatial profile of excitation in response to a localized stimulus. Georg von Békésy, in his book Sensory Inhibition, explores a wide range of inhibitory phenomena in sensory systems, and interprets them in terms of sharpening.
Mach bands	The illusion consists of light or dark stripes that are perceived next to the boundary between two regions of an image that have different lightness gradients (even if the lightness itself is the same on both sides of the boundary). The Mach bands effect is due to the spatial high-boost filtering performed by the human visual system on the luminance channel of the image captured by the retina. This filtering is largely performed in the retina itself, by lateral inhibition among its neurons.
Complex cell	Complex cells can be found in the primary visual cortex (V1), the secondary visual cortex (V2), and Brodmann area 19 (V3) . Like a simple cell, a complex cell will respond primarily to oriented edges and gratings, however it has a degree of spatial invariance. This means that its receptive field cannot be mapped into fixed excitatory and inhibitory zones.
Ocular dominance column	Ocular dominance columns are stripes of neurons in the visual cortex of certain mammals (including humans) that respond preferentially to input from one eye or the other. The columns span multiple cortical layers, and are laid out in a striped pattern across the surface of the striate cortex (V1). The stripes lie perpendicular to the orientation columns.
Sine	In mathematics, the sine function is a function of an angle. In a right triangle, sine gives the ratio of the length of the side opposite to an angle to the length of the hypotenuse. Sine is usually listed first amongst the trigonometric functions.
Fourier analysis	In mathematics, Fourier analysis is a subject area which grew from the study of Fourier series. The subject began with the study of the way general functions may be represented by sums of simpler trigonometric functions. Fourier analysis is named after Joseph Fourier, who showed that representing a function by a trigonometric series greatly simplifies the study of heat propagation.
Color vision	Color vision is the capacity of an organism or machine to distinguish objects based on the wavelengths (or frequencies) of the light they reflect, emit, or transmit.

Chapter 6. The Visual System

	The nervous system derives color by comparing the responses to light from the several types of cone photoreceptors in the eye. These cone photoreceptors are sensitive to different portions of the visible spectrum.
Complementary color	Complementary colors are pairs of colors that are of 'opposite' hue in some color model. The exact hue 'complementary' to a given hue depends on the model in question, and perceptually uniform, additive, and subtractive color models, for example, have differing complements for any given color. Color theory In color theory, two colors are called complementary if, when mixed in the proper proportion, they produce a neutral color (grey, white, or black).
Color constancy	Color constancy is an example of subjective constancy and a feature of the human color perception system which ensures that the perceived color of objects remains relatively constant under varying illumination conditions. A green apple for instance looks green to us at midday, when the main illumination is white sunlight, and also at sunset, when the main illumination is red. This helps us identify objects.

1. _____ refers to the difference in image location of an object seen by the left and right eyes, resulting from the eyes' horizontal separation. The brain uses _____ to extract depth information from the two-dimensional retinal images in stereopsis. In computer vision, _____ refers to the difference in coordinates of similar features within two stereo images.

    a. Binocular disparity
    b. Binocular summation
    c. Binocular vision
    d. Blind spot

2. . _____s are pairs of colors that are of 'opposite' hue in some color model. The exact hue 'complementary' to a given hue depends on the model in question, and perceptually uniform, additive, and subtractive color models, for example, have differing complements for any given color.

    Color theory

In color theory, two colors are called complementary if, when mixed in the proper proportion, they produce a neutral color (grey, white, or black).

a. Demosaicing
b. Complementary color
c. Dichromatism
d. DispcalGUI

3. _____ is an attribute of visual perception in which a source appears to be radiating or reflecting light. In other words, _____ is the perception elicited by the luminance of a visual target. This is a subjective attribute/property of an object being observed.

a. Lightness
b. Camera exposure settings
c. Brightness
d. massed learning

4. _____, is a biological pigment of the retina that is responsible for both the formation of the photoreceptor cells and the first events in the perception of light. _____s belong to the G-protein coupled receptor family and are extremely sensitive to light, enabling vision in low-light conditions. Exposed to light, the pigment immediately photobleaches, and it takes about 30 minutes to regenerate fully in humans.

a. Pigment dispersion syndrome
b. Pupillary response
c. Carl Rogers theory evaluation
d. Rhodopsin

5. _____ is the capacity of an organism or machine to distinguish objects based on the wavelengths (or frequencies) of the light they reflect, emit, or transmit. The nervous system derives color by comparing the responses to light from the several types of cone photoreceptors in the eye. These cone photoreceptors are sensitive to different portions of the visible spectrum.

a. Gaze-contingency paradigm
b. Glob
c. Color vision
d. Pareidolia

1. a
2. b
3. c
4. d
5. c

You can take the complete Chapter Practice Test

for Chapter 6. The Visual System
on all key terms, persons, places, and concepts.

Online 99 Cents

http://www.epub3.10.9241.6.cram101.com/

Use www.Cram101.com for all your study needs

including Cram101's online interactive problem solving labs in

chemistry, statistics, mathematics, and more.

Chapter 7. Mechanisms of Perception, Conscious Awareness, and Attention

Sensory cortex

Sensory system

Simultanagnosia

Prosopagnosia

Sensation

Binding problem

Parallel processing

Blindness

Posterior parietal cortex

Scotoma

Visual cortex

Blindsight

Agnosia

Fusiform face area

Cochlea

Eardrum

Fourier analysis

Organ of Corti

Ossicles

	Stapes
	Sine
	Basilar membrane
	Semicircular canal
	Tectorial membrane
	Primary auditory cortex
	Round window
	Vestibular system
	Sound localization
	Free nerve ending
	Bulbous corpuscle
	Anterolateral system
	Dermatome
	Medial lemniscus
	Secondary somatosensory cortex
	Ventral posterior nucleus
	Spinoreticular tract
	Spinotectal tract
	Spinothalamic tract

Thalamus

Anosognosia

Anterior cingulate cortex

Cingulate cortex

Endorphin

Hemispherectomy

Lobotomy

Neuropeptide

Periaqueductal gray

Olfaction

Raphe nuclei

Olfactory bulb

Olfactory mucosa

Orbitofrontal cortex

Piriform cortex

Taste bud

Anosmia

Solitary nucleus

Solitary

	Change blindness

CHAPTER HIGHLIGHTS & NOTES: KEY TERMS, PEOPLE, PLACES, CONCEPTS

Sensory cortex	The sensory cortex can refer informally to the primary somatosensory cortex, on left and right hemisphere): the visual cortex on the occipital lobes, the auditory cortex on the temporal lobes, the primary olfactory cortex on the uncus of the piriform region of the temporal lobes, the gustatory cortex on the insular lobe (also referred to as the insular cortex), and the primary somatosensory cortex on the anterior parietal lobes. Just posterior to the primary somatosensory cortex lies the somatosensory association cortex, which integrates sensory information from the primary somatosensory cortex. to construct an understanding of the object being felt.
Sensory system	A sensory system is a part of the nervous system responsible for processing sensory information. A sensory system consists of sensory receptors, neural pathways, and parts of the brain involved in sensory perception. Commonly recognized sensory systems are those for vision, hearing, somatic sensation (touch), taste and olfaction (smell).
Simultanagnosia	Simultanagnosia is a rare neurological disorder characterized by the inability of an individual to perceive more than a single object at a time. It is one of three major components of Bálint's syndrome, an uncommon and incompletely understood variety of severe neuropsychological impairments involving space representation (visuospatial processing). The term 'simultanagnosia' was first coined in 1924 by Wolpert to describe a condition where the affected individual could see individual details of a complex scene but failed to grasp the overall meaning of the image.
Prosopagnosia	Prosopagnosia is a disorder of face perception where the ability to recognize faces is impaired, while the ability to recognize other objects may be relatively intact. The term originally referred to a condition following acute brain damage, but a congenital form of the disorder has been proposed, which may be inherited by about 2.5% of the population. The specific brain area usually associated with prosopagnosia is the fusiform gyrus.
Sensation	In psychology, sensation and perception are stages of processing of the senses in human and animal systems, such as vision, auditory, vestibular, and pain senses.

Chapter 7. Mechanisms of Perception, Conscious Awareness, and Attention

	These topics are considered part of psychology, and not anatomy or physiology, because processes in the brain so greatly affect the perception of a stimulus. Included in this topic is the study of illusions such as motion aftereffect, color constancy, auditory illusions, and depth perception.
Binding problem	The binding problem is one of a number of terms at the interface between neuroscience and philosophy which suffer from being used in several different ways, often in a context that does not explicitly indicate which way the term is being used. Of the many possible usages, two common versions may be useful anchor points. Firstly, there is the practical issue of how brains segregate elements in complex patterns of data.
Parallel processing	Parallel processing is the ability to carry out multiple operations or tasks simultaneously. The term is used in the contexts of both human cognition, particularly in the ability of the brain to simultaneously process incoming stimuli, and in parallel computing by machines. Parallel processing is the ability of the brain to simultaneously process incoming stimuli of differing quality.
Blindness	Blindness is the condition of lacking visual perception due to physiological or neurological factors. Various scales have been developed to describe the extent of vision loss and define blindness. Total blindness is the complete lack of form and visual light perception and is clinically recorded as NLP, an abbreviation for 'no light perception.' Blindness is frequently used to describe severe visual impairment with residual vision.
Posterior parietal cortex	The posterior parietal cortex plays an important role in producing planned movements. Before an effective movement can be initiated, the nervous system must know the original positions of the body parts that are to be moved, and the positions of any external objects with which the body is going to interact. The posterior parietal cortex receives input from the three sensory systems that play roles in the localization of the body and external objects in space: the visual system, the auditory system, and the somatosensory system.
Scotoma	A scotoma is an area of partial alteration in one's field of vision consisting of a partially diminished or entirely degenerated visual acuity which is surrounded by a field of normal - or relatively well-preserved - vision. Every normal mammalian eye has a scotoma in its field of vision, usually termed its blind spot. This is a location with no photoreceptor cells, where the retinal ganglion cell axons that comprise the optic nerve exit the retina.

Visual cortex	The visual cortex of the brain is the part of the cerebral cortex responsible for processing visual information. It is located in the occipital lobe, in the back of the brain. The term visual cortex refers to the primary visual cortex and extrastriate visual cortical areas such as V2, V3, V4, and V5. The primary visual cortex is anatomically equivalent to Brodmann area 17, or BA17. The extrastriate cortical areas consist of Brodmann area 18 and Brodmann area 19.
Blindsight	Blindsight is a phenomenon in which people who are perceptually blind in a certain area of their visual field demonstrate some response to visual stimuli. In Type 1 blindsight subjects have no awareness whatsoever of any stimuli, but yet are able to predict, at levels significantly above chance, aspects of a visual stimulus, such as location, or type of movement, often in a forced-response or guessing situation. Type 2 blindsight is when subjects have some awareness of, for example, movement within the blind area, but no visual percept.
Agnosia	Agnosia is a loss of ability to recognize objects, persons, sounds, shapes, or smells while the specific sense is not defective nor is there any significant memory loss. It is usually associated with brain injury or neurological illness, particularly after damage to the occipitotemporal border, which is part of the ventral stream.
Fusiform face area	The fusiform face area is a part of the human visual system which might be specialized for facial recognition, although there is some evidence that it also processes categorical information about other objects, particularly familiar ones. It is located in the fusiform gyrus (Brodmann area 37). Localization The Fusiform face area is located in the ventral stream on the ventral surface of the temporal lobe on the lateral side of the fusiform gyrus.
Cochlea	The cochlea is the auditory portion of the inner ear. It is a spiral-shaped cavity in the bony labyrinth, in humans making 2.5 turns around its axis, the modiolus. A core component of the cochlea is the Organ of Corti, the sensory organ of hearing, which is distributed along the partition separating fluid chambers in the coiled tapered tube of the cochlea.
Eardrum	The eardrum, is a thin, cone-shaped membrane that separates the external ear from the middle ear in humans and other tetrapods. Its function is to transmit sound from the air to the ossicles inside the middle ear. The malleus bone bridges the gap between the eardrum and the other ossicles.
Fourier analysis	In mathematics, Fourier analysis is a subject area which grew from the study of Fourier series. The subject began with the study of the way general functions may be represented by sums of simpler trigonometric functions.

Chapter 7. Mechanisms of Perception, Conscious Awareness, and Attention

Organ of Corti	The organ of Corti is the organ in the inner ear found only in mammals that contains auditory sensory cells, or 'hair cells.' The organ of Corti has highly specialized structures that respond to fluid-borne vibrations in the cochlea with a shearing vector in the hairs of some cochlear hair cells. It contains between 15,000-20,000 auditory nerve receptors. Each receptor has its own hair cell.
Ossicles	The ossicles are the three smallest bones in the human body. They are contained within the middle ear space and serve to transmit sounds from the air to the fluid-filled labyrinth (cochlea). The absence of the auditory ossicles would constitute a moderate-to-severe hearing loss.
Stapes	The stapes is attached through the incudostapedial joint to the incus laterally and to the fenestra ovalis, the 'oval window', medially. The oval window is adjacent to the vestibule of the inner ear. The stapes is the smallest and lightest bone in the human body.
Sine	In mathematics, the sine function is a function of an angle. In a right triangle, sine gives the ratio of the length of the side opposite to an angle to the length of the hypotenuse. Sine is usually listed first amongst the trigonometric functions.
Basilar membrane	The basilar membrane within the cochlea of the inner ear is a stiff structural element that separates two liquid-filled tubes that run along the coil of the cochlea, the scala media and the scala tympani . Endolymph/perilymph separation The fluids in these two tubes, the endolymph and the perilymph are very different chemically, biochemically, and electrically. Therefore they are kept strictly separated.
Semicircular canal	The semicircular canals are three half-circular, interconnected tubes located inside each ear. The three canals are the horizontal semicircular canal superior semicircular canal and the posterior semicircular canal. The canals are aligned approximately orthogonally to one another.
Tectorial membrane	Covering the sulcus spiralis internus and the spiral organ of Corti in the cochlea is the tectorial membrane, which is attached to the limbus laminae spiralis (spiral limbus) close to the inner edge of the vestibular membrane. The tectorial membrane covers the hair cells in Organ of Corti, with the longer hairs of the outer hair cells embedded in it. The membrane itself is a gel-like structure containing at three different glycoproteins; α-tectorin, β-tectorin and otogelin.
Primary auditory cortex	The primary auditory cortex is a region of the brain that processes sound and thereby contributes to our ability to hear. It is the first cortical region of the auditory pathway.

Round window	The round window is one of the two openings into the inner ear. It is closed off from the middle ear by the round window membrane, which vibrates with opposite phase to vibrations entering the inner ear through the oval window. It allows fluid in the cochlea to move, which in turn ensures that hair cells of the basilar membrane will be stimulated and that audition will occur.
Vestibular system	The vestibular system, which contributes to balance in most mammals and to the sense of spatial orientation, is the sensory system that provides the leading contribution about movement and sense of balance. Together with the cochlea, a part of the auditory system, it constitutes the labyrinth of the inner ear in most mammals, situated in the vestibulum in the inner ear. As movements consist of rotations and translations, the vestibular system comprises two components: the semicircular canal system, which indicate rotational movements; and the otoliths, which indicate linear accelerations.
Sound localization	Sound localization refers to a listener's ability to identify the location or origin of a detected sound in direction and distance. It may also refer to the methods in acoustical engineering to simulate the placement of an auditory cue in a virtual 3D space .
	The sound localization mechanisms of the human auditory system have been extensively studied.
Free nerve ending	A free nerve ending is an unspecialized, afferent nerve ending, meaning it brings information from the body's periphery toward the brain. They function as cutaneous receptors and are essentially used by vertebrates to detect pain.
	Structure
	Free nerve endings are unencapsulated and have no complex sensory structures, unlike those found in Meissner's or Pacinian corpuscles.
Bulbous corpuscle	The Bulbous corpuscle is a class of slowly adapting mechanoreceptor thought to exist only in the glabrous dermis and subcutaneous tissue of humans. It is named after Angelo Ruffini.
	Function
	This spindle-shaped receptor is sensitive to skin stretch, and contributes to the kinesthetic sense of and control of finger position and movement.
Anterolateral system	In the nervous system, the anterolateral system is an ascending pathway that conveys pain, temperature (protopathic sensation), and crude touch from the periphery to the brain.
Dermatome	A dermatome is an area of skin that is mainly supplied by a single spinal nerve.

	There are eight cervical nerves (C1 being an exception with no dermatome), twelve thoracic nerves, five lumbar nerves and five sacral nerves. Each of these nerves relays sensation (including pain) from a particular region of skin to the brain.
Medial lemniscus	The medial lemniscus, is a pathway in the brainstem that carries sensory information from the gracile and cuneate nuclei to the thalamus. Path After neurons carrying proprioceptive or touch information synapse at the gracile and cuneate nuclei, axons from secondary neurons decussate at the level of the medulla and travel up the brainstem as the medial lemniscus on the contralateral (opposite) side. It is part of the posterior column-medial lemniscus system, which transmits touch, vibration sense, as well as the pathway for proprioception.
Secondary somatosensory cortex	The human secondary somatosensory cortex is a region of cerebral cortex lying mostly on the parietal operculum. Region S2 was first described by Adrian in 1940, who found that feeling in cats' feet was not only represented in the previously described primary somatosensory cortex (S1) but also in a second region adjacent to S1. In 1954, Penfield and Jasper evoked somatosensory sensations in human patients during neurosurgery using electrical stimulation in the lateral sulcus, which lies adjacent to S1, and their findings were confirmed in 1979 by Woolsey et al. using evoked potentials and electrical stimulation. Functional neuroimaging studies have found S2 activation in response to light touch, pain, visceral sensation, and tactile attention.
Ventral posterior nucleus	The ventral posterior nucleus is the somato-sensory relay nucleus in thalamus of the brain. Input and output The ventral posterior nucleus receives neuronal input from the medial lemniscus, spinal lemniscus, spinothalamic tracts, and trigeminothalamic tract. It projects to the somatosensory cortex and the ascending reticuloactivation system.
Spinoreticular tract	The spinoreticular tract is an ascending pathway in the white matter of the spinal cord, positioned closely to the lateral spinothalamic tract. The tract is from spinal cord---to reticular formation--- to thalamus. It is responsible for automatic responses to pain, such as in the case of injury.
Spinotectal tract	The spinotectal tract arises in the anterolateral column and terminate in the inferior and superior colliculi.

	It is situated ventral to the lateral spinothalamic fasciculus, but its fibers are more or less intermingled with it.
	It is also known as the spino-quadrigeminal system of Mott.
Spinothalamic tract	The spinothalamic tract is a sensory pathway originating in the spinal cord. It is one component of the anterolateral system. It transmits information to the thalamus about pain, temperature, itch and crude touch.
Thalamus	The thalamus is a midline symmetrical structure within the brains of vertebrates including humans, situated between the cerebral cortex and midbrain. Its function includes relaying sensory and motor signals to the cerebral cortex, along with the regulation of consciousness, sleep, and alertness. The thalamus surrounds the third ventricle.
Anosognosia	Anosognosia is viewed as a deficit of self-awareness, a condition in which a person who suffers certain disability seems unaware of the existence of his or her disability. It was first named by the neurologist, Joseph Babinski, in 1914. Unlike denial, which is a psychological defence mechanism, anosognosia results from physiological damage on brain structures, typically to the parietal lobe or a diffused lesion on the fronto-temporal-parietal area in the right hemisphere. Causes
	Relatively little has been discovered about the cause of the condition since its initial identification.
Anterior cingulate cortex	The anterior cingulate cortex is the frontal part of the cingulate cortex, that resembles a 'collar' form around the corpus callosum. It consists of Brodmann areas 24, 32 and 33. It appears to play a role in a wide variety of autonomic functions, such as regulating blood pressure and heart rate, as well as rational cognitive functions, such as reward anticipation, decision-making, empathy and emotion. Anatomy
	The anterior cingulate cortex can be divided anatomically based on cognitive (dorsal), and emotional (ventral) components.
Cingulate cortex	The cingulate cortex is a part of the brain situated in the medial aspect of the cortex. It includes the cortex of the cingulate gyrus, which lies immediately above the corpus callosum, and the continuation of this in the cingulate sulcus. The cingulate cortex is usually considered part of the limbic lobe.
Endorphin	Endorphins ('endogenous morphine') are endogenous opioid peptides that function as neurotransmitters.

	They are produced by the pituitary gland and the hypothalamus in vertebrates during exercise, excitement, pain, consumption of spicy food, love and orgasm, and they resemble the opiates in their abilities to produce analgesia and a feeling of well-being.
	The term implies a pharmacological activity (analogous to the activity of the corticosteroid category of biochemicals) as opposed to a specific chemical formulation.
Hemispherectomy	Hemispherectomy is a very rare surgical procedure where one cerebral hemisphere (half of the brain) is removed or disabled. This procedure is used to treat a variety of seizure disorders where the source of the epilepsy is localized to a broad area of a single hemisphere of the brain, among other disorders. It is solely reserved for extreme cases in which the seizures have not responded to medications and other less invasive surgeries.
Lobotomy	Lobotomy (Greek: λοβ?ς - lobos: 'lobe (of brain)'; τομ? - tome: 'cut/slice') is a neurosurgical procedure, a form of psychosurgery, also known as a leukotomy or leucotomy . It consists of cutting the connections to and from the prefrontal cortex, the anterior part of the frontal lobes of the brain. While the procedure, initially termed a leucotomy, has been controversial since its inception in 1935, it was a mainstream procedure for more than two decades, prescribed for psychiatric (and occasionally other) conditions--this despite general recognition of frequent and serious side-effects.
Neuropeptide	Neuropeptides are small protein-like molecules used by neurons to communicate with each other, distinct from the larger neurotransmitters. They are neuronal signaling molecules, influence the activity of the brain in specific ways and are thus involved in particular brain functions, like analgesia, reward, food intake, learning and memory.
	Neuropeptides are expressed and released by neurons, and mediate or modulate neuronal communication by acting on cell surface receptors.
Periaqueductal gray	Periaqueductal gray is the gray matter located around the cerebral aqueduct within the tegmentum of the midbrain. It plays a role in the descending modulation of pain and in defensive behaviour. The ascending pain and temperature fibers of the spinothalamic tract also send information to the PAG via the spinomesencephalic tract .
Olfaction	Olfaction is the sense of smell. This sense is mediated by specialized sensory cells of the nasal cavity of vertebrates, and, by analogy, sensory cells of the antennae of invertebrates. Many vertebrates, including most mammals and reptiles, have two distinct olfactory systems--the main olfactory system, and the accessory olfactory system (mainly used to detect pheremones).
Raphe nuclei	The raphe nuclei are a moderate-size cluster of nuclei found in the brain stem. Their main function is to release serotonin to the rest of the brain.

Olfactory bulb	The olfactory bulb is a structure of the vertebrate forebrain involved in olfaction, the perception of odors.
	In most vertebrates, the olfactory bulb is the most rostral (forward) part of the brain. In humans, however, the olfactory bulb is on the inferior (bottom) side of the brain.
Olfactory mucosa	The olfactory mucosa is located in the upper region of the nasal cavity and is made up of the olfactory epithelium and the underlying lamina propria, connective tissue containing fibroblasts, blood vessels, Bowman's glands and bundles of fine axons from the olfactory neurons.
	The mucus protects the olfactory epithelium and allows odors to dissolve so that they can be detected by olfactory receptor neurons. Electron microscopy studies show that Bowman's glands contain cells with large secretory vesicles.
Orbitofrontal cortex	The orbitofrontal cortex is a prefrontal cortex region in the frontal lobes in the brain which is involved in the cognitive processing of decision-making. In non-human primates it consists of the association cortex areas Brodmann area 11, 12 and 13; in humans it consists of Brodmann area 10, 11 and 47 Because of its functions in emotion and reward, the OFC is considered by some to be a part of the limbic system.
	The OFC anatomically is defined as the part of the prefrontal cortex that receives projections from the magnocellular, medial nucleus of the mediodorsal thalamus.
Piriform cortex	In anatomy of animals, the piriform cortex is a region in the brain.
	The piriform cortex is part of the rhinencephalon situated in the telencephalon.
	In human anatomy, the 'piriform lobe' has been described as consisting of the cortical amygdala, uncus, and anterior parahippocampal gyrus.
Taste bud	Taste buds contain the receptors for taste. They are located around the small structures on the upper surface of the tongue, soft palate, upper esophagus and epiglottis, which are called papillae. These structures are involved in detecting the five (known) elements of taste perception: salty, sour, bitter, sweet, and savory.
Anosmia	Anosmia is a lack of functioning olfaction, or in other words, an inability to perceive odors. Anosmia may be temporary but traumatic anosmia can be permanent. Anosmia is not due to any inflammation of the nasal mucosa; blockage of nasal passages or a destruction of one temporal lobe.

Chapter 7. Mechanisms of Perception, Conscious Awareness, and Attention

Solitary nucleus	In the human brain, the solitary nucleus is a series of nuclei (clusters of nerve cell bodies) forming a vertical column of grey matter embedded in the medulla oblongata. Through the center of the NTS runs the solitary tract, a white bundle of nerve fibers, including fibers from the facial, glossopharyngeal and vagus nerves that synapse on neurons of the NTS. The NTS projects to, among other regions, the reticular formation, parasympathetic preganglionic neurons, hypothalamus and thalamus, forming circuits that contribute to autonomic regulation. Cells within the NTS are arranged according to function; for instance, cells involved in taste are located in the higher, more forward ('rostral') part, while those regulating cardio-respiratory processes are found in the lower, more posterior ('caudal') part.
Solitary	Solitude is a state of being alone. Territorial Animals that are solitary are often territorial and do not like the company of another animal in their territory and especially an animal of their own kind. This could be due to competition between rivals for the opportunity to mate or over territory, or it could be a more suitable way to live in the environment.
Change blindness	Change blindness is a psychological phenomenon that occurs when a change in a visual stimulus goes unnoticed by the observer. For example, an individual fails to notice a difference between two images that are identical except for one change. The reasons these changes usually remain unnoticed by the observer include obstructions in the visual field, eye movements, a change of location, or a lack of attention.

1. The _____ is a structure of the vertebrate forebrain involved in olfaction, the perception of odors.

   In most vertebrates, the _____ is the most rostral (forward) part of the brain. In humans, however, the _____ is on the inferior (bottom) side of the brain.

   a. Olfactory bulb
   b. Archicortex
   c. Islands of Calleja
   d. Region IV of hippocampus proper

2. . The _____ is a part of the brain situated in the medial aspect of the cortex. It includes the cortex of the cingulate gyrus, which lies immediately above the corpus callosum, and the continuation of this in the cingulate sulcus. The _____ is usually considered part of the limbic lobe.

a. Carl Rogers theory evaluation

b. Anterolateral corticospinal tract

c. Apical dendrite

d. Cingulate cortex

3. The _____ is a sensory pathway originating in the spinal cord. It is one component of the anterolateral system. It transmits information to the thalamus about pain, temperature, itch and crude touch.

a. Type Ia sensory fiber

b. Type II sensory fiber

c. Spinothalamic tract

d. Carl Rogers theory evaluation

4. Solitude is a state of being alone.

Territorial

Animals that are _____ are often territorial and do not like the company of another animal in their territory and especially an animal of their own kind. This could be due to competition between rivals for the opportunity to mate or over territory, or it could be a more suitable way to live in the environment.

a. Solitary animal

b. Challenging behaviour

c. Solitary

d. Horse behavior

5. The _____ is the frontal part of the cingulate cortex, that resembles a 'collar' form around the corpus callosum. It consists of Brodmann areas 24, 32 and 33. It appears to play a role in a wide variety of autonomic functions, such as regulating blood pressure and heart rate, as well as rational cognitive functions, such as reward anticipation, decision-making, empathy and emotion. Anatomy

The _____ can be divided anatomically based on cognitive (dorsal), and emotional (ventral) components.

a. Anterior gray column

b. Anterior cingulate cortex

c. Apical dendrite

d. Automated Anatomical Labeling

1. a
2. d
3. c
4. c
5. b

You can take the complete Chapter Practice Test

for Chapter 7. Mechanisms of Perception, Conscious Awareness, and Attention
on all key terms, persons, places, and concepts.

Online 99 Cents

http://www.epub3.10.9241.7.cram101.com/

Use www.Cram101.com for all your study needs

including Cram101's online interactive problem solving labs in

chemistry, statistics, mathematics, and more.

Chapter 8. The Sensorimotor System

_____ | Posterior parietal cortex

_____ | Apraxia

_____ | Premotor cortex

_____ | Supplementary motor area

_____ | Basal ganglia

_____ | Cerebellum

_____ | Betz cell

_____ | Red nucleus

_____ | Vestibular nuclei

_____ | Acetylcholine

_____ | Motor pool

_____ | Motor unit

_____ | Muscle spindle

_____ | Renshaw cell

_____ | Chunking

_____ | Ebbinghaus illusion

_____ | Secondary somatosensory cortex

Posterior parietal cortex	The posterior parietal cortex plays an important role in producing planned movements. Before an effective movement can be initiated, the nervous system must know the original positions of the body parts that are to be moved, and the positions of any external objects with which the body is going to interact. The posterior parietal cortex receives input from the three sensory systems that play roles in the localization of the body and external objects in space: the visual system, the auditory system, and the somatosensory system.
Apraxia	Apraxia is characterized by loss of the ability to execute or carry out learned purposeful movements, despite having the desire and the physical ability to perform the movements. It is a disorder of motor planning, which may be acquired or developmental, but is not caused by incoordination, sensory loss, or failure to comprehend simple commands (which can be tested by asking the person to recognize the correct movement from a series). It is caused by damage to specific areas of the cerebrum.
Premotor cortex	The premotor cortex is an area of motor cortex lying within the frontal lobe of the brain just anterior to the primary motor cortex. It occupies part of Broadman's area 6. It has been studied mainly in primates, including monkeys and humans. The functions of the premotor cortex are diverse and not fully understood.
Supplementary motor area	The supplementary motor area is a part of the sensorimotor cerebral cortex (perirolandic, i.e. on each side of the Rolando or central sulcus). It was included, on purely cytoarchitectonic arguments, in area 6 of Brodmann and the Vogts. It is located on the medial face of the hemisphere, just in front of primary motor cortex.
Basal ganglia	The basal ganglia are a group of nuclei of varied origin in the brains of vertebrates that act as a cohesive functional unit. They are situated at the base of the forebrain and are strongly connected with the cerebral cortex, thalamus and other brain areas. The basal ganglia are associated with a variety of functions, including voluntary motor control, procedural learning relating to routine behaviors or 'habits' such as bruxism, eye movements, and cognitive, emotional functions.
Cerebellum	The cerebellum is a region of the brain that plays an important role in motor control. It is also involved in some cognitive functions such as attention and language, and probably in some emotional functions such as regulating fear and pleasure responses. Its movement-related functions are the most clearly understood, however.
Betz cell	Betz cells are large pyramidal cell neurons located within the fifth layer of the grey matter in the primary motor cortex, M1. They are named after Vladimir Alekseyevich Betz, who described them in his work published in 1874. These neurons are the largest in the central nervous system, sometimes reaching 100 μm in diameter.

	Betz cells send their axons down to the spinal cord where in humans they synapse directly with anterior horn cells, which in turn synapse directly with their target muscles. While Betz cells have one apical dendrite typical to pyramidal neurons, they have more primary dendritic shafts, and these do not leave the soma only at basal angles but rather branch out from almost any point asymmetrically.
Red nucleus	The red nucleus is a structure in the rostral midbrain involved in motor coordination. It comprises a caudal magnocellular and a rostral parvocellular part. It is located in the tegmentum of the midbrain next to the substantia nigra.
Vestibular nuclei	The vestibular nuclei are the cranial nuclei for the vestibular nerve.

In Terminologia Anatomica they are grouped in both the pons and medulla. Subnuclei

There are 4 subnuclei; they are situated at the floor of the fourth ventricle. |
| Acetylcholine | The chemical compound acetylcholine is a neurotransmitter in both the peripheral nervous system (PNS) and central nervous system (CNS) in many organisms including humans. Acetylcholine is one of many neurotransmitters in the autonomic nervous system (ANS) and the only neurotransmitter used in the motor division of the somatic nervous system. (Sensory neurons use glutamate and various peptides at their synapses). Acetylcholine is also the principal neurotransmitter in all autonomic ganglia. |
| Motor pool | In neuroscience, a motor pool refers to a group of motor spinal neurons that innervate the same muscle. The biological significance of motor pool organization is in the fact that motor pools with many neurons produce finer movements. For example, the motor unit of muscles in the torso will control more muscle fibers and so cannot discriminate and selectively contract one particular fiber over another. |
| Motor unit | A motor unit is made up of a motor neuron and the skeletal muscle fibers innervated by that axon. Groups of motor units often work together to coordinate the contractions of a single muscle; all of the motor units within a muscle are considered a motor pool.

All muscle fibers in a motor unit will be of the same fiber type. |
| Muscle spindle | Muscle spindles are sensory receptors within the belly of a muscle, which primarily detect changes in the length of this muscle. They convey length information to the central nervous system via sensory neurons. This information can be processed by the brain to determine the position of body parts. |

Renshaw cell	Renshaw cells are inhibitory interneurons found in the gray matter of the spinal cord, and are associated in two ways with an alpha motor neuron. •They receive an excitatory collateral from the alpha neuron's axon as they emerge from the motor root, and are thus 'kept informed' of how vigorously that neuron is firing.•They send an inhibitory axon to synapse with the cell body of the initial alpha neuron and/or an alpha motor neuron of the same motor pool. In this way, Renshaw cell inhibition represents a negative feedback mechanism. A Renshaw cell may be supplied by more than one alpha motor neuron collateral and it may synapse on multiple motor neurons.
Chunking	In mathematics education at primary school level, chunking (sometimes also called the partial quotients method) is an elementary approach for solving simple division questions, by repeated subtraction. To calculate the result of dividing a large number by a small number, the student repeatedly takes away 'chunks' of the large number, where each 'chunk' is an easy multiple (for example 100×, 10×, 5× 2×, etc). of the small number, until the large number has been reduced to zero or the remainder is less than the divisor.
Ebbinghaus illusion	The Ebbinghaus illusion is an optical illusion of relative size perception. In the best-known version of the illusion, two circles of identical size are placed near to each other and one is surrounded by large circles while the other is surrounded by small circles; the first central circle then appears smaller than the second central circle. It was named for its discoverer, the German psychologist Hermann Ebbinghaus (1850-1909) it was popularised in the English-speaking world by Titchener in a 1901 textbook of experimental psychology, hence its alternative name 'Titchener circles'.
Secondary somatosensory cortex	The human secondary somatosensory cortex is a region of cerebral cortex lying mostly on the parietal operculum. Region S2 was first described by Adrian in 1940, who found that feeling in cats' feet was not only represented in the previously described primary somatosensory cortex (S1) but also in a second region adjacent to S1. In 1954, Penfield and Jasper evoked somatosensory sensations in human patients during neurosurgery using electrical stimulation in the lateral sulcus, which lies adjacent to S1, and their findings were confirmed in 1979 by Woolsey et al. using evoked potentials and electrical stimulation. Functional neuroimaging studies have found S2 activation in response to light touch, pain, visceral sensation, and tactile attention.

Chapter 8. The Sensorimotor System

1. The _____ plays an important role in producing planned movements. Before an effective movement can be initiated, the nervous system must know the original positions of the body parts that are to be moved, and the positions of any external objects with which the body is going to interact. The _____ receives input from the three sensory systems that play roles in the localization of the body and external objects in space: the visual system, the auditory system, and the somatosensory system.

   a. Prefrontal cortex
   b. Posterior parietal cortex
   c. Proisocortex
   d. Putamen

2. In mathematics education at primary school level, _____ (sometimes also called the partial quotients method) is an elementary approach for solving simple division questions, by repeated subtraction.

   To calculate the result of dividing a large number by a small number, the student repeatedly takes away 'chunks' of the large number, where each 'chunk' is an easy multiple (for example 100×, 10×, 5× 2×, etc). of the small number, until the large number has been reduced to zero or the remainder is less than the divisor.

   a. Cube
   b. Chunking
   c. Division by two
   d. Finger binary

3. The _____ is a structure in the rostral midbrain involved in motor coordination. It comprises a caudal magnocellular and a rostral parvocellular part. It is located in the tegmentum of the midbrain next to the substantia nigra.

   a. massed learning
   b. Brodmann area
   c. Calcarine fissure
   d. Red nucleus

4. The _____ are the cranial nuclei for the vestibular nerve.

   In Terminologia Anatomica they are grouped in both the pons and medulla. Subnuclei

   There are 4 subnuclei; they are situated at the floor of the fourth ventricle.

   a. Carl Rogers theory evaluation
   b. Brodmann area
   c. Vestibular nuclei
   d. Cerebral aqueduct

5. _____s are sensory receptors within the belly of a muscle, which primarily detect changes in the length of this muscle. They convey length information to the central nervous system via sensory neurons. This information can be processed by the brain to determine the position of body parts.

    a. Merkel nerve ending
    b. Near-death experience
    c. Neural backpropagation
    d. Muscle spindle

1. b
2. b
3. d
4. c
5. d

You can take the complete Chapter Practice Test

for Chapter 8. The Sensorimotor System
on all key terms, persons, places, and concepts.

Online 99 Cents

http://www.epub3.10.9241.8.cram101.com/

Use www.Cram101.com for all your study needs

including Cram101's online interactive problem solving labs in

chemistry, statistics, mathematics, and more.

Chapter 9. Development of the Nervous System

CHAPTER OUTLINE: KEY TERMS, PEOPLE, PLACES, CONCEPTS

	Zygote
	Neural groove
	Neural plate
	Aggregation
	Cerebral hemisphere
	Mesencephalon
	Neural crest
	Radial glial cell
	Cerebrum
	Axon
	Growth cone
	Optic nerve
	Retinal ganglion cell
	Glial cell
	Astrocyte
	Synaptogenesis
	Apoptosis
	Necrosis
	Nerve growth factor

	Dendrite
	Perseveration
	Working memory
	Monocular deprivation
	Absolute pitch
	Neurogenesis
	Neuroplasticity
	Tinnitus
	Williams syndrome
	Spatial cognition

CHAPTER HIGHLIGHTS & NOTES: KEY TERMS, PEOPLE, PLACES, CONCEPTS

Zygote	A zygote is the initial cell formed when a new organism is produced by means of sexual reproduction. A zygote is synthesized from the union of two gametes, and constitutes the first stage in a unique organism's development. Zygotes are usually produced by a fertilization event between two haploid cells--an ovum from a female and a sperm cell from a male--which combine to form the single diploid cell.
Neural groove	The neural groove is a shallow median groove between the neural folds of an embryo. The neural folds are two longitudinal ridges that are caused by a folding up of the ectoderm in front of the primitive streak of the developing embryo.

| Neural plate | In human embryology, formation of neural plate is the first step of neurulation. It is created by a flat thickening opposite to the primitive streak of the ectoderm.

Development

During the stage of neural plate formation the embryo consists of three cell layers: the previously mentioned ectoderm that eventually forms the skin and neural tissues, the mesoderm that forms muscle and bone, and the endoderm that will form the cells lining the digestive and respiratory tract. |
| --- | --- |
| Aggregation | Aggregation is a subtask of natural language generation, which involves merging syntactic constituents (such as sentences and phrases) together. Sometimes aggregation is also done at a conceptual level.

A simple example of syntactic aggregation is merging the two sentences John went to the shop and John bought an apple into the single sentence John went to the shop and bought an apple. |
| Cerebral hemisphere | A cerebral hemisphere is one of the two regions of the eutherian brain that are delineated by the median plane, (medial longitudinal fissure). The brain can thus be described as being divided into left and right cerebral hemispheres. Each of these hemispheres has an outer layer of grey matter called the cerebral cortex that is supported by an inner layer of white matter. |
| Mesencephalon | In biological anatomy, the mesencephalon (or midbrain) comprises the tectum (or corpora quadrigemina), tegmentum, the ventricular mesocoelia (or 'iter'), and the cerebral peduncles, as well as several nuclei and fasciculi. Caudally the mesencephalon adjoins the pons (metencephalon) and rostrally it adjoins the diencephalon (Thalamus, hypothalamus, et al)..

During development, the mesencephalon forms from the middle of three vesicles that arise from the neural tube to generate the brain. |
| Neural crest | Neural crest cells are a transient, multipotent, migratory cell population unique to vertebrates that gives rise to a diverse cell lineage including melanocytes, craniofacial cartilage and bone, smooth muscle, peripheral and enteric neurons and glia.

After gastrulation, neural crest cells are specified at the border of the neural plate and the non-neural ectoderm. During neurulation, the borders of the neural plate, also known as the neural folds, converge at the dorsal midline to form the neural tube. |
| Radial glial cell | Radial glial cells are a pivotal cell type in the developing central nervous system (CNS) involved in key developmental processes, from patterning and neuronal migration to their recently discovered role as precursors during neurogenesis. |

	They arise early in development from neuroepithelial cells. Radial phenotype is typically transient, but some cells, such as Bergmann glia in the cerebellum and Muller glia in the retina, retain radial glia-like morphology postnatally.
Cerebrum	The cerebrum, together with the diencephalon, constitutes the forebrain. In humans, the cerebrum is the most superior region of the vertebrate central nervous system. However, in the majority of animals, the cerebrum is the most anterior region of the CNS as the anatomical position of animals is rarely in the upright position.
Axon	An axon is a long, slender projection of a nerve cell, or neuron, that typically conducts electrical impulses away from the neuron's cell body. In certain sensory neurons (pseudounipolar neurons), such as those for touch and warmth, the electrical impulse travels along an axon from the periphery to the cell body, and from the cell body to the spinal cord along another branch of the same axon. Axon dysfunction causes many inherited and acquired neurological disorders which can affect both the peripheral and central neurons.
Growth cone	A growth cone is a dynamic, actin-supported extension of a developing axon seeking its synaptic target. Their existence was originally proposed by Spanish histologist Santiago Ramón y Cajal based upon stationary images he observed under the microscope. He first described the growth cone based on fixed cells as 'a concentration of protoplasm of conical form, endowed with amoeboid movements' (Cajal, 1890).
Optic nerve	The optic nerve, transmits visual information from the retina to the brain. Derived from the embryonic retinal ganglion cell, a diverticulum located in the diencephalon, the optic nerve does not regenerate after transection. The optic nerve is the second of twelve paired cranial nerves but is considered to be part of the central nervous system, as it is derived from an outpouching of the diencephalon during embryonic development.
Retinal ganglion cell	A retinal ganglion cell is a type of neuron located near the inner surface (the ganglion cell layer) of the retina of the eye. It receives visual information from photoreceptors via two intermediate neuron types: bipolar cells and amacrine cells. Retinal ganglion cells collectively transmit image-forming and non-image forming visual information from the retina to several regions in the thalamus, hypothalamus, and mesencephalon, or midbrain.
Glial cell	Glial cells are non-neuronal cells that maintain homeostasis, form myelin, and provide support and protection for the brain's neurons. In the human brain, there is roughly one glia for every neuron with a ratio of about two neurons for every three glia in the cerebral gray matter.
Astrocyte	Astrocytes (etymology: astron gk. star, cyte gk.

Synaptogenesis	Synaptogenesis is the formation of synapses. Although it occurs throughout a healthy person's lifespan, an explosion of synapse formation occurs during early brain development. Synaptogenesis is particularly important during an individual's 'critical period' of life, during which there is a certain degree of neuronal pruning due to competition for neural growth factors by neurons and synapses.
Apoptosis	Apoptosis is the process of programmed cell death (PCD) that may occur in multicellular organisms. Biochemical events lead to characteristic cell changes (morphology) and death. These changes include blebbing, cell shrinkage, nuclear fragmentation, chromatin condensation, and chromosomal DNA fragmentation.
Necrosis	Necrosis is the premature death of cells in living tissue. Necrosis is caused by factors external to the cell or tissue, such as infection, toxins, or trauma. This is in contrast to apoptosis, which is a naturally occurring cause of cellular death.
Nerve growth factor	Nerve growth factor is a small secreted protein that is important for the growth, maintenance, and survival of certain target neurons (nerve cells). It also functions as a signaling molecule. It is perhaps the prototypical growth factor, in that it is one of the first to be described.
Dendrite	Dendrites are the branched projections of a neuron that act to conduct the electrochemical stimulation received from other neural cells to the cell body, or soma, of the neuron from which the dendrites project. Electrical stimulation is transmitted onto dendrites by upstream neurons via synapses which are located at various points throughout the dendritic arbor. Dendrites play a critical role in integrating these synaptic inputs and in determining the extent to which action potentials are produced by the neuron.
Perseveration	Perseveration is the repetition of a particular response, such as a word, phrase, or gesture, despite the absence or cessation of a stimulus, usually caused by brain injury or other organic disorder. If an issue has been fully explored and discussed to a point of resolution, it is not uncommon for something to trigger the re-investigation of the matter. This can happen at any time during a conversation. This is particularly true with those who have had traumatic brain injuries.
Working memory	Working memory has been defined as the system which actively holds information in the mind to do verbal and nonverbal tasks such as reasoning and comprehension, and to make it available for further information processing. Working memory tasks are those that require the goal-oriented active monitoring or manipulation of information or behaviors in the face of interfering processes and distractions. Working memory can only retain a limited amount of information; however, its capacity can be increased by use of a method known as chunking.

Chapter 9. Development of the Nervous System

Monocular deprivation	Monocular deprivation is an experimental technique used by neuroscientists to study central nervous system plasticity. Generally, one of an animal's eyes is sutured shut during a period of high cortical plasticity (4-5 weeks-old in mice (Gordon 1997)). This manipulation serves as an animal model for amblyopia, a permanent deficit in visual sensation not due to abnormalities in the eye .
Absolute pitch	Absolute pitch widely referred to as perfect pitch, is the ability of a person to identify or re-create a given musical note without the benefit of an external reference. Absolute pitch or perfect pitch, is the ability to name or reproduce a tone without reference to an external standard. Correct identification of the pitch need not be expressed linguistically; AP can also be demonstrated in auditory imagery or sensorimotor responses, for example by reproducing on an instrument a tone that has been heard (without 'hunting' for the correct pitch).
Neurogenesis	Neurogenesis is the process by which neurons are generated from neural stem and progenitor cells. Most active during pre-natal development, neurogenesis is responsible for populating the growing brain with neurons. Recently neurogenesis was shown to continue in several small parts of the brain of mammals: the hippocampus and the subventricular zone.
Neuroplasticity	Neuroplasticity refers to the susceptibility to physiological changes of the nervous system, due to changes in behavior, environment, neural processes, or parts of the body other than the nervous system. The brain changes throughout life. Neuroplasticity occurs on a variety of levels, ranging from cellular changes due to learning, to large-scale changes involved in cortical remapping in response to injury.
Tinnitus	Tinnitus is the perception of sound within the human ear in the absence of corresponding external sound. Tinnitus is not a disease, but a symptom that can result from a wide range of underlying causes: abnormally loud sounds in the ear canal for even the briefest period (but usually with some duration), ear infections, foreign objects in the ear, nose allergies that prevent (or induce) fluid drain, or wax build-up. Withdrawal from a benzodiazepine addiction may cause tinnitus as well.
Williams syndrome	Williams syndrome is a rare neurodevelopmental disorder caused by a deletion of about 26 genes from the long arm of chromosome 7. It is characterized by a distinctive, 'elfin' facial appearance, along with a low nasal bridge; an unusually cheerful demeanor and ease with strangers; developmental delay coupled with unusual (for persons who are diagnosed as developmentally delayed) language skills; and cardiovascular problems, such as supravalvular aortic stenosis and transient hypercalcaemia. The syndrome was first identified in 1961 by Dr. J. C. P.

| Spatial cognition | Spatial cognition is concerned with the acquisition, organization, utilization, and revision of knowledge about spatial environments. These capabilities enable humans to manage basic and high-level cognitive tasks in everyday life. Numerous disciplines (such as Psychology, Geographic Information Science, Artificial Intelligence, Cartography, etc). |

1. _____s (etymology: astron gk. star, cyte gk. cell), also known collectively as astroglia, are characteristic star-shaped glial cells in the brain and spinal cord.

   a. Axon terminal
   b. Endoneurium
   c. Epineurium
   d. Astrocyte

2. _____ is the process of programmed cell death (PCD) that may occur in multicellular organisms. Biochemical events lead to characteristic cell changes (morphology) and death. These changes include blebbing, cell shrinkage, nuclear fragmentation, chromatin condensation, and chromosomal DNA fragmentation.

   a. Apoptosis
   b. Asystole
   c. Ataxic respiration
   d. Beating heart cadaver

3. _____ is a rare neurodevelopmental disorder caused by a deletion of about 26 genes from the long arm of chromosome 7. It is characterized by a distinctive, 'elfin' facial appearance, along with a low nasal bridge; an unusually cheerful demeanor and ease with strangers; developmental delay coupled with unusual (for persons who are diagnosed as developmentally delayed) language skills; and cardiovascular problems, such as supravalvular aortic stenosis and transient hypercalcaemia. The syndrome was first identified in 1961 by Dr. J. C. P. Williams of New Zealand and has an estimated prevalence of 1 in 7,500 to 1 in 20,000 births.

   a. Neuromyelitis optica
   b. Glanzmann's thrombasthenia
   c. rat-bite fever
   d. Williams syndrome

4. . _____ refers to the susceptibility to physiological changes of the nervous system, due to changes in behavior, environment, neural processes, or parts of the body other than the nervous system. The brain changes throughout life.

_____ occurs on a variety of levels, ranging from cellular changes due to learning, to large-scale changes involved in cortical remapping in response to injury.

a. Neuropsychophysiology
b. Neuroradiology
c. Neurorehabilitation
d. Neuroplasticity

5. _____ cells are a transient, multipotent, migratory cell population unique to vertebrates that gives rise to a diverse cell lineage including melanocytes, craniofacial cartilage and bone, smooth muscle, peripheral and enteric neurons and glia.

After gastrulation, _____ cells are specified at the border of the neural plate and the non-neural ectoderm. During neurulation, the borders of the neural plate, also known as the neural folds, converge at the dorsal midline to form the neural tube.

a. Neural crest
b. diencephalon
c. Carl Rogers theory evaluation
d. Primary motor cortex

1. d

2. a

3. d

4. d

5. a

You can take the complete Chapter Practice Test

for Chapter 9. Development of the Nervous System
on all key terms, persons, places, and concepts.

Online 99 Cents

http://www.epub3.10.9241.9.cram101.com/

Use www.Cram101.com for all your study needs

including Cram101's online interactive problem solving labs in

chemistry, statistics, mathematics, and more.

Chapter 10. Brain Damage and Neuroplasticity

CHAPTER OUTLINE: KEY TERMS, PEOPLE, PLACES, CONCEPTS

_____	Brain damage
_____	Brain tumor
_____	Neoplasm
_____	NMDA receptor
_____	Dementia
_____	Subgaleal hemorrhage
_____	Mumps
_____	Tardive dyskinesia
_____	Apoptosis
_____	Down syndrome
_____	Necrosis
_____	Phenylketonuria
_____	Convulsion
_____	Epilepsy
_____	Focal epilepsy
_____	Partial seizure
_____	Cerebral hypoxia
_____	Complex partial seizure
_____	Temporal lobe epilepsy

Mutation

Nigrostriatal pathway

Parkinson's disease

Substantia nigra

Alzheimer's disease

Ataxia

Epidemiology

Multiple sclerosis

Remyelination

Amygdala

Entorhinal cortex

Neurofibrillary tangle

Posterior parietal cortex

Acetylcholine

Epileptogenesis

Kindling model

Axotomy

Schwann cell

Transneuronal degeneration

	Neuroplasticity
	Cerebral edema
	Edema
	Cognitive reserve
	Neurogenesis
	Estrogen
	Nerve growth factor
	Ischemia
	Spinal cord
	Phantom limb

CHAPTER HIGHLIGHTS & NOTES: KEY TERMS, PEOPLE, PLACES, CONCEPTS

Brain damage	Brain damage is the destruction or degeneration of brain cells. Brain injuries occur due to a wide range of internal and external factors. A common category with the greatest number of injuries is traumatic brain injury (TBI) following physical trauma or head injury from an outside source, and the term acquired brain injury (ABI) is used in appropriate circles, to differentiate brain injuries occurring after birth, from injury due to a disorder or congenital malady.
Brain tumor	A brain tumor is an intracranial solid neoplasm, a tumor (defined as an abnormal growth of cells) within the brain or the central spinal canal. Brain tumors include all tumors inside the cranium or in the central spinal canal.

Chapter 10. Brain Damage and Neuroplasticity

Neoplasm	Neoplasm is an abnormal mass of tissue as a result of neoplasia. Neoplasia is the abnormal proliferation of cells. The growth of neoplastic cells exceeds and is uncoordinated with that of the normal tissues around it. The growth persists in the same excessive manner even after cessation of the stimuli. It usually causes a lump or tumor. Neoplasms may be benign, pre-malignant (carcinoma in situ) or malignant (cancer).
NMDA receptor	The NMDA receptor a glutamate receptor, is the predominant molecular device for controlling synaptic plasticity and memory function. The NMDAR is a specific type of ionotropic glutamate receptor. NMDA (N-methyl-D-aspartate) is the name of a selective agonist that binds to NMDA receptors but not to other glutamate receptors.
Dementia	Dementia is a serious loss of global cognitive ability in a previously unimpaired person, beyond what might be expected from normal aging. It may be static, the result of a unique global brain injury, or progressive, resulting in long-term decline due to damage or disease in the body. Although dementia is far more common in the geriatric population, it can occur before the age of 65, in which case it is termed 'early onset dementia'.
Subgaleal hemorrhage	Subgaleal hemorrhage is bleeding in the potential space between the skull periosteum and the scalp galea aponeurosis. Majority (90%) result from vacuum applied to the head at delivery (Ventouse assisted delivery). The vacuum assist ruptures the emissary veins (connections between dural sinus and scalp veins) leading to accumulation of blood under the aponeurosis of the scalp muscle and superficial to the periosteum.
Mumps	Mumps is a viral disease of the human species, caused by the mumps virus. Before the development of vaccination and the introduction of a vaccine, it was a common childhood disease worldwide. It is still a significant threat to health in the third world, and outbreaks still occur sporadically in developed countries.
Tardive dyskinesia	Tardive dyskinesia is a difficult-to-treat form of dyskinesia (disorder resulting in involuntary, repetitive body movements) that can be tardive (having a slow or belated onset). It frequently appears after long-term or high-dose use of antipsychotic drugs, or in children and infants as a side effect from usage of drugs for gastrointestinal disorders prevention. Tardive dyskinesia is characterized by repetitive, involuntary, purposeless movements, such as grimacing, tongue protrusion, lip smacking, puckering and pursing of the lips, and rapid eye blinking.

Apoptosis	Apoptosis is the process of programmed cell death (PCD) that may occur in multicellular organisms. Biochemical events lead to characteristic cell changes (morphology) and death. These changes include blebbing, cell shrinkage, nuclear fragmentation, chromatin condensation, and chromosomal DNA fragmentation.
Down syndrome	Down syndrome, also known as trisomy 21, is a chromosomal condition caused by the presence of all or part of a third copy of chromosome 21. Down syndrome is the most common chromosome abnormality in humans. It is typically associated with a delay in cognitive ability (mental retardation, or MR) and physical growth, and a particular set of facial characteristics. The average IQ of young adults with Down syndrome is around 50, compared to children without the condition with an IQ of 100. (MR has historically been defined as an IQ below 70).
Necrosis	Necrosis is the premature death of cells in living tissue. Necrosis is caused by factors external to the cell or tissue, such as infection, toxins, or trauma. This is in contrast to apoptosis, which is a naturally occurring cause of cellular death.
Phenylketonuria	Phenylketonuria is an autosomal recessive metabolic genetic disorder characterized by a mutation in the gene for the hepatic enzyme phenylalanine hydroxylase (PAH), rendering it nonfunctional. This enzyme is necessary to metabolize the amino acid phenylalanine (Phe) to the amino acid tyrosine. When PAH activity is reduced, phenylalanine accumulates and is converted into phenylpyruvate (also known as phenylketone), which is detected in the urine.
Convulsion	A convulsion is a medical condition where body muscles contract and relax rapidly and repeatedly, resulting in an uncontrolled shaking of the body. Because a convulsion is often a symptom of an epileptic seizure, the term convulsion is sometimes used as a synonym for seizure. However, not all epileptic seizures lead to convulsions, and not all convulsions are caused by epileptic seizures.
Epilepsy	Epilepsy is a common and diverse set of chronic neurological disorders characterized by seizures. Some definitions of epilepsy require that seizures be recurrent and unprovoked, but others require only a single seizure combined with brain alterations which increase the chance of future seizures. In many cases a cause cannot be identified; however, factors that are associated include brain trauma, strokes, brain cancer, and drug and alcohol misuse among others.
Focal epilepsy	Focal epilepsy, is a seizure disorder in which seizures are preceded by an isolated disturbance of a cerebral function. Such disturbances may include a twitching of a part of the body, such as a limb; a deceptive or illusory sensation or feeling, or some other mental disturbance. It is a subtype of epilepsy.

Chapter 10. Brain Damage and Neuroplasticity

Partial seizure	Partial seizures (also called focal seizures and localized seizures) are seizures which affect only a part of the brain at onset. The brain is divided into two hemispheres, each consisting of four lobes - the frontal, temporal, parietal and occipital lobes. In partial seizures the seizure is generated in and affects just one part of the brain - the whole hemisphere or part of a lobe.
Cerebral hypoxia	Cerebral hypoxia refers to a reduced supply of oxygen to the brain. Cerebral anoxia refers to a complete lack of oxygen to the brain. There are four categories of cerebral hypoxia; in order of severity they are; diffuse cerebral hypoxia focal cerebral ischemia, cerebral infarction, and global cerebral ischemia.
Complex partial seizure	A complex partial seizure is an epileptic seizure that is associated with bilateral cerebral hemisphere involvement and causes impairment of awareness or responsiveness, i.e. loss of consciousness.
Temporal lobe epilepsy	Temporal lobe epilepsy a.k.a. Psychomotor epilepsy, is a form of focal epilepsy, a chronic neurological condition characterized by recurrent seizures. Over 40 types of epilepsies are known. They fall into two main categories: partial-onset (focal or localization-related) epilepsies and generalized-onset epilepsies.
Mutation	In molecular biology and genetics, mutations are changes in a genomic sequence: the DNA sequence of a cell's genome or the DNA or RNA sequence of a virus. These random sequences can be defined as sudden and spontaneous changes in the cell. Mutations are caused by radiation, viruses, transposons and mutagenic chemicals, as well as errors that occur during meiosis or DNA replication.
Nigrostriatal pathway	Dopaminergic pathways are neural pathways in the brain which transmit the neurotransmitter dopamine from one region of the brain to another. The nigrostriatal pathway is a neural pathway that connects the substantia nigra with the striatum. It is one of the four major dopamine pathways in the brain, and is particularly involved in the production of movement, as part of a system called the basal ganglia motor loop.
Parkinson's disease	Parkinson's disease is a degenerative disorder of the central nervous system. It results from the death of dopamine-containing cells in the substantia nigra, a region of the midbrain; the cause of cell-death is unknown. Early in the course of the disease, the most obvious symptoms are movement-related, including shaking, rigidity, slowness of movement and difficulty with walking and gait. Later, cognitive and behavioural problems may arise, with dementia commonly occurring in the advanced stages of the disease. Other symptoms include sensory, sleep and emotional problems. Parkinson's disease is more common in the elderly with most cases occurring after the age of 50.

Substantia nigra	The substantia nigra is a brain structure located in the mesencephalon (midbrain) that plays an important role in reward, addiction, and movement. Substantia nigra is Latin for 'black substance', as parts of the substantia nigra appear darker than neighboring areas due to high levels of melanin in dopaminergic neurons. Parkinson's disease is caused by the death of dopaminergic neurons in the substantia nigra pars compacta.
Alzheimer's disease	Alzheimer's disease also called Alzheimer disease, senile dementia of the Alzheimer type, primary degenerative dementia of the Alzheimer's type, or simply Alzheimer's, is the most common form of dementia. This incurable, degenerative, and terminal disease was first described by German psychiatrist and neuropathologist Alois Alzheimer in 1906 and was named after him. Most often, it is diagnosed in people over 65 years of age, although the less-prevalent early-onset Alzheimer's can occur much earlier.
Ataxia	Ataxia is a neurological sign and symptom that consists of gross lack of coordination of muscle movements. Ataxia is a non-specific clinical manifestation implying dysfunction of the parts of the nervous system that coordinate movement, such as the cerebellum. Several possible causes exist for these patterns of neurological dysfunction.
Epidemiology	Epidemiology is the study of disease patterns in a society. It is the cornerstone method of public health research, and helps inform evidence-based medicine for identifying risk factors for disease and determining optimal treatment approaches to clinical practice and for preventive medicine. In the study of communicable and non-communicable diseases, epidemiologists are involved in outbreak investigation to study design, data collection, statistical analysis, documentation of results and submission for publication.
Multiple sclerosis	Multiple sclerosis is an inflammatory disease in which the fatty myelin sheaths around the axons of the brain and spinal cord are damaged, leading to demyelination and scarring as well as a broad spectrum of signs and symptoms. Disease onset usually occurs in young adults, and it is more common in females. It has a prevalence that ranges between 2 and 150 per 100,000. multiple sclerosis was first described in 1868 by Jean-Martin Charcot.
Remyelination	Remyelination is a term for the re-generation of the nerve's myelin sheath, damaged in many diseases such as multiple sclerosis (MS) and the leukodystrophies. Remyelination is a subject of active medical research.
Amygdala	The are almond-shaped groups of nuclei located deep within the medial temporal lobes of the brain in complex vertebrates, including humans. Shown in research to perform a primary role in the processing of memory and emotional reactions, the amygdalae are considered part of the limbic system. Anatomical subdivisions

Chapter 10. Brain Damage and Neuroplasticity

Entorhinal cortex	The entorhinal cortex (ento = interior, rhino = nose, entorinal = interior to the rhinal sulcus). is located in the medial temporal lobe and functions as a hub in a widespread network for memory and navigation. The EC is the main interface between the hippocampus and neocortex.
Neurofibrillary tangle	Neurofibrillary Tangles (NFTs) are aggregates of hyperphosphorylated tau protein that are most commonly known as a primary marker of Alzheimer's Disease. Their presence is also found in numerous other diseases known as Tauopathies. Little is known about their exact relationship to the different pathologies.
Posterior parietal cortex	The posterior parietal cortex plays an important role in producing planned movements. Before an effective movement can be initiated, the nervous system must know the original positions of the body parts that are to be moved, and the positions of any external objects with which the body is going to interact. The posterior parietal cortex receives input from the three sensory systems that play roles in the localization of the body and external objects in space: the visual system, the auditory system, and the somatosensory system.
Acetylcholine	The chemical compound acetylcholine is a neurotransmitter in both the peripheral nervous system (PNS) and central nervous system (CNS) in many organisms including humans. Acetylcholine is one of many neurotransmitters in the autonomic nervous system (ANS) and the only neurotransmitter used in the motor division of the somatic nervous system. (Sensory neurons use glutamate and various peptides at their synapses). Acetylcholine is also the principal neurotransmitter in all autonomic ganglia.
Epileptogenesis	Epileptogenesis is a process by which a normal brain develops epilepsy, a chronic condition in which seizures occur. The process, which is gradual, occurs in symptomatic epilepsy, in which seizures are caused by an identifiable lesion in the brain. It results from acute brain insults such as traumatic brain injury (physical trauma to the brain), stroke, or infection.
Kindling model	Kindling is a commonly used model for the development of seizures and epilepsy in which the duration and behavioral involvement of induced seizures increases after seizures are induced repeatedly. The kindling model was first proposed in the late 1960s by Goddard and colleagues. Although kindling is a widely used model, its applicability to human epilepsy is controversial.
Axotomy	An axotomy is the cutting or otherwise severing of an axon. Derived from axo- (=axon) and -tomy (=surgery). This type of denervation is often used in experimental studies on neuronal physiology and neuronal death or survival as a method to better understand nervous system diseases.
Schwann cell	Schwann cells or neurolemmocytes are the principal glia of the peripheral nervous system (PNS).

Glial cells function to support neurons and in the PNS, also include satellite cells, olfactory ensheathing cells, enteric glia and glia that reside at sensory nerve endings, such as the Pacinian corpuscle. There are two types of Schwann cell, myelinating and nonmyelinating.

Transneuronal degeneration	Transneuronal degeneration is the death of neurons resulting from the disruption of input from or output to other nearby neurons.
Neuroplasticity	Neuroplasticity refers to the susceptibility to physiological changes of the nervous system, due to changes in behavior, environment, neural processes, or parts of the body other than the nervous system. The brain changes throughout life. Neuroplasticity occurs on a variety of levels, ranging from cellular changes due to learning, to large-scale changes involved in cortical remapping in response to injury.
Cerebral edema	Cerebral edema is an excess accumulation of water in the intracellular or extracellular spaces of the brain. Four types of cerebral edema have been distinguished:Vasogenic Due to a breakdown of tight endothelial junctions which make up the blood-brain barrier (BBB). This allows normally excluded intravascular proteins and fluid to penetrate into cerebral parenchymal extracellular space.
Edema	Edema, formerly known as dropsy or hydropsy, is an abnormal accumulation of fluid beneath the skin or in one or more cavities of the body. Generally, the amount of interstitial fluid is determined by the balance of fluid homeostasis, and increased secretion of fluid into the interstitium or impaired removal of this fluid may cause edema. Classification Cutaneous edema is referred to as 'pitting' when after pressure is applied to a small area, the indentation persists for some time after the release of the pressure.
Cognitive reserve	The term cognitive reserve describes the mind's resilience to neuropathological damage of the brain. The mind's resilience is evaluated behaviorally, whereas the neuropathological damage is evaluated histologically, although damage may be estimated using blood-based markers and imaging methods. There are two models that can be used when exploring the concept of 'reserve': brain reserve and cognitive reserve.
Neurogenesis	Neurogenesis is the process by which neurons are generated from neural stem and progenitor cells.

Chapter 10. Brain Damage and Neuroplasticity

	Most active during pre-natal development, neurogenesis is responsible for populating the growing brain with neurons. Recently neurogenesis was shown to continue in several small parts of the brain of mammals: the hippocampus and the subventricular zone.
Estrogen	Estrogens (AmE), oestrogens , are a group of compounds named for their importance in the estrous cycle of humans and other animals, and functioning as the primary female sex hormones. Natural estrogens are steroid hormones, while some synthetic ones are non-steroidal.
Nerve growth factor	Nerve growth factor is a small secreted protein that is important for the growth, maintenance, and survival of certain target neurons (nerve cells). It also functions as a signaling molecule. It is perhaps the prototypical growth factor, in that it is one of the first to be described.
Ischemia	In medicine, ischemia, also spelled as ischaemia or ischæmia, is a restriction in blood supply to tissues, causing a shortage of oxygen and glucose needed for cellular metabolism (to keep tissue alive). Ischemia is generally caused by problems with blood vessels, with resultant damage or dysfunction of tissue. It also means local anemia in a given part of a body sometimes resulting from congestion (such as vasoconstriction, thrombosis or embolism).
Spinal cord	The spinal cord is a long, thin, tubular bundle of nervous tissue and support cells that extends from the brain (the medulla oblongata specifically). The brain and spinal cord together make up the central nervous system (CNS). The spinal cord begins at the occipital bone and extends down to the space between the first and second lumbar vertebrae; it does not extend the entire length of the vertebral column.
Phantom limb	A phantom limb is the sensation that an amputated or missing limb (even an organ, like the appendix) is still attached to the body and is moving appropriately with other body parts. Approximately 60 to 80% of individuals with an amputation experience phantom sensations in their amputated limb, and the majority of the sensations are painful. Phantom sensations may also occur after the removal of body parts other than the limbs, e.g. after amputation of the breast, extraction of a tooth (phantom tooth pain) or removal of an eye (phantom eye syndrome).

1. _____ is the study of disease patterns in a society. It is the cornerstone method of public health research, and helps inform evidence-based medicine for identifying risk factors for disease and determining optimal treatment approaches to clinical practice and for preventive medicine. In the study of communicable and non-communicable diseases, epidemiologists are involved in outbreak investigation to study design, data collection, statistical analysis, documentation of results and submission for publication.

   a. Organized Crime Control Act
   b. Asia Society
   c. Epidemiology
   d. Aeron chair

2. _____ is a small secreted protein that is important for the growth, maintenance, and survival of certain target neurons (nerve cells). It also functions as a signaling molecule. It is perhaps the prototypical growth factor, in that it is one of the first to be described.

   a. Nerve growth factor
   b. Neurodevelopmental disorder
   c. Neuroepithelial cell
   d. Neurotrophin-3

3. _____ is an abnormal mass of tissue as a result of neoplasia. Neoplasia is the abnormal proliferation of cells. The growth of neoplastic cells exceeds and is uncoordinated with that of the normal tissues around it. The growth persists in the same excessive manner even after cessation of the stimuli. It usually causes a lump or tumor. _____s may be benign, pre-malignant (carcinoma in situ) or malignant (cancer).

   a. Marjolin's ulcer
   b. Neoplasm
   c. Bone marrow suppression
   d. Pagetoid

4. _____ is bleeding in the potential space between the skull periosteum and the scalp galea aponeurosis.

   Majority (90%) result from vacuum applied to the head at delivery (Ventouse assisted delivery). The vacuum assist ruptures the emissary veins (connections between dural sinus and scalp veins) leading to accumulation of blood under the aponeurosis of the scalp muscle and superficial to the periosteum.

   a. Suboccipital puncture
   b. Subgaleal hemorrhage
   c. Tardive dysmentia
   d. Tarlov cyst

5. . _____ is the destruction or degeneration of brain cells. Brain injuries occur due to a wide range of internal and external factors.

Chapter 10. Brain Damage and Neuroplasticity

A common category with the greatest number of injuries is traumatic brain injury (TBI) following physical trauma or head injury from an outside source, and the term acquired brain injury (ABI) is used in appropriate circles, to differentiate brain injuries occurring after birth, from injury due to a disorder or congenital malady.

a. Carl Rogers theory evaluation
b. massed learning
c. Posse Comitatus Act
d. Brain damage

1. c
2. a
3. b
4. b
5. d

Electroencephalography

Lobotomy

Olfactory bulb

Optic chiasm

Retrograde amnesia

Temporal lobe

Amnesia

Epilepsy

Anterograde amnesia

Digit Span

Classical conditioning

Episodic memory

Explicit memory

Implicit memory

Memory consolidation

Mnemonic

Semantic memory

Korsakoff's syndrome

Dementia

Chapter 11. Learning, Memory, and Amnesia

CHAPTER OUTLINE: KEY TERMS, PEOPLE, PLACES, CONCEPTS

- Acetylcholine
- Basal forebrain
- Coma
- Basal
- Brain damage
- Engram
- Hippocampus
- Place cell
- Spatial memory
- Working memory
- Sensory cortex
- Neuroplasticity
- Prefrontal cortex
- Long-term potentiation
- NMDA receptor
- Dendritic spine

CHAPTER HIGHLIGHTS & NOTES: KEY TERMS, PEOPLE, PLACES, CONCEPTS

Electroencephalography	Electroencephalography is the recording of electrical activity along the scalp. EEG measures voltage fluctuations resulting from ionic current flows within the neurons of the brain. In clinical contexts, EEG refers to the recording of the brain's spontaneous electrical activity over a short period of time, usually 20-40 minutes, as recorded from multiple electrodes placed on the scalp.
Lobotomy	Lobotomy (Greek: λοβ?ς - lobos: 'lobe (of brain)'; τομ? - tome: 'cut/slice') is a neurosurgical procedure, a form of psychosurgery, also known as a leukotomy or leucotomy . It consists of cutting the connections to and from the prefrontal cortex, the anterior part of the frontal lobes of the brain. While the procedure, initially termed a leucotomy, has been controversial since its inception in 1935, it was a mainstream procedure for more than two decades, prescribed for psychiatric (and occasionally other) conditions--this despite general recognition of frequent and serious side-effects.
Olfactory bulb	The olfactory bulb is a structure of the vertebrate forebrain involved in olfaction, the perception of odors.

In most vertebrates, the olfactory bulb is the most rostral (forward) part of the brain. In humans, however, the olfactory bulb is on the inferior (bottom) side of the brain. |
| Optic chiasm | The optic chiasm is the part of the brain where the optic nerves (CN II) partially cross. The optic chiasm is located at the bottom of the brain immediately below the hypothalamus.

The images on the nasal sides of each retina cross over to the opposite side of the brain via the optic nerve at the optic chiasm. |
| Retrograde amnesia | Retrograde amnesia is a loss of access to events that occurred, or information that was learned, before an injury or the onset of a disease. RA is often temporally graded, consistent with Ribot's Law: more recent memories closer to the traumatic incident are more likely to be forgotten than more remote memories.

The most commonly affected areas are associated with episodic and declarative memory such as the hippocampus, the diencephalon, and the temporal lobes. |
| Temporal lobe | The temporal lobe is a region of the cerebral cortex that is located beneath the Sylvian fissure on both cerebral hemispheres of the mammalian brain.

The temporal lobe is involved in auditory perception and is home to the primary auditory cortex. It is also important for the processing of semantics in both speech and vision. The temporal lobe contains the hippocampus and plays a key role in the formation of long-term memory. |
| Amnesia | Amnesia is a condition in which one's memory is lost. |

Chapter 11. Learning, Memory, and Amnesia

	The causes of amnesia have traditionally been divided into certain categories. Memory appears to be stored in several parts of the limbic system of the brain, and any condition that interferes with the function of this system can cause amnesia.
Epilepsy	Epilepsy is a common and diverse set of chronic neurological disorders characterized by seizures. Some definitions of epilepsy require that seizures be recurrent and unprovoked, but others require only a single seizure combined with brain alterations which increase the chance of future seizures. In many cases a cause cannot be identified; however, factors that are associated include brain trauma, strokes, brain cancer, and drug and alcohol misuse among others.
Anterograde amnesia	Anterograde amnesia is a loss of the ability to create new memories after the event that caused the amnesia, leading to a partial or complete inability to recall the recent past, while long-term memories from before the event remain intact. This is in contrast to retrograde amnesia, where memories created prior to the event are lost. Both can occur together in the same patient.
Digit Span	In psychology and neuroscience, memory span is the longest list of items that a person can repeat back in correct order immediately after presentation on 50% of all trials. Items may include words, numbers, or letters. The task is known as digit span when numbers are used.
Classical conditioning	Classical conditioning is a form of learning in which the conditioned stimulus or CS, comes to signal the occurrence of a second stimulus, the unconditioned stimulus or US. (A stimulus is a factor that causes a response in an organism). The US is usually a biologically significant stimulus such as food or pain that elicits a response from the start; this is called the unconditioned response or UR. The CS usually produces no particular response at first, but after conditioning it elicits the conditioned response or CR. Classical conditioning differs from operant or instrumental conditioning, in which behavior emitted by the subject is strengthened or weakened by its consequences (i.e. reward or punishment).

Conditioning is usually done by pairing the two stimuli, as in Pavlov's classic experiments. |
| Episodic memory | Episodic memory is the memory of autobiographical events (times, places, associated emotions, and other contextual knowledge) that can be explicitly stated. Semantic and episodic memory together make up the category of declarative memory, which is one of the two major divisions in memory. The counterpart to declarative, or explicit memory, is procedural memory, or implicit memory. |
| Explicit memory | Explicit memory is the conscious, intentional recollection of previous experiences and information. People use explicit memory throughout the day, such as remembering the time of an appointment or recollecting an event from years ago. |

Implicit memory	Implicit memory is a type of memory in which previous experiences aid in the performance of a task without conscious awareness of these previous experiences. Evidence for implicit memory arises in priming, a process whereby subjects are measured by how they have improved their performance on tasks for which they have been subconsciously prepared. Implicit memory also leads to the illusion-of-truth effect, which suggests that subjects are more likely to rate as true those statements that they have already heard, regardless of their veracity.
Memory consolidation	Memory consolidation is a category of processes that stabilize a memory trace after the initial acquisition. Consolidation is distinguished into two specific processes, synaptic consolidation, which occurs within the first few hours after learning, and system consolidation, where hippocampus-dependent memories become independent of the hippocampus over a period of weeks to years. Recently, a third process has become the focus of research, reconsolidation, in which previously consolidated memories can be made labile again through reactivation of the memory trace.
Mnemonic	A mnemonic device, is any learning technique that aids information retention. Mnemonics aim to translate information into a form that the human brain can retain better and even the process of applying this conversion might already aid the transfer of information to long-term memory. Commonly encountered mnemonics are often for lists and in auditory form, such as short poems, acronyms, or memorable phrases, but mnemonics can also be for other types of information and in visual or kinesthetic forms.
Semantic memory	Semantic memory refers to the memory of meanings, understandings, and other concept-based knowledge unrelated to specific experiences. The conscious recollection of factual information and general knowledge about the world is generally thought to be independent of context and personal relevance. Semantic and episodic memory together make up the category of declarative memory, which is one of the two major divisions in memory.
Korsakoff's syndrome	Korsakoff's syndrome is a neurological disorder caused by the lack of thiamine (vitamin B_1) in the brain. Its onset is linked to chronic alcohol abuse and/or severe malnutrition. The syndrome is named after Sergei Korsakoff, the neuropsychiatrist who popularized the theory.
Dementia	Dementia is a serious loss of global cognitive ability in a previously unimpaired person, beyond what might be expected from normal aging. It may be static, the result of a unique global brain injury, or progressive, resulting in long-term decline due to damage or disease in the body. Although dementia is far more common in the geriatric population, it can occur before the age of 65, in which case it is termed 'early onset dementia'.
Acetylcholine	The chemical compound acetylcholine is a neurotransmitter in both the peripheral nervous system (PNS) and central nervous system (CNS) in many organisms including humans.

Chapter 11. Learning, Memory, and Amnesia

	Acetylcholine is one of many neurotransmitters in the autonomic nervous system (ANS) and the only neurotransmitter used in the motor division of the somatic nervous system. (Sensory neurons use glutamate and various peptides at their synapses). Acetylcholine is also the principal neurotransmitter in all autonomic ganglia.
Basal forebrain	The basal forebrain is a collection of structures located ventrally to the striatum. It is considered to be the major cholinergic output of the central nervous system (CNS). It includes a group of structures that lie near the bottom of the front of the brain, including the nucleus basalis, diagonal band of Broca, and medial septal nuclei.
Coma	In medicine, a coma is a state of unconsciousness, lasting more than six hours in which a person cannot be awakened, fails to respond normally to painful stimuli, light, sound, lacks a normal sleep-wake cycle and does not initiate voluntary actions. A person in a state of coma is described as comatose. Although, according to the Glasgow Coma Scale, a person with confusion is considered to be in the mildest coma.
Basal	In phylogenetics, a basal clade is the earliest clade to branch in a larger clade; it appears at the base of a cladogram. A basal group forms an outgroup to the rest of the clade, such as in the following example: The word 'basal' is preferred to the term 'primitive', which may carry false connotations of inferiority or a lack of complexity. The term basal can only be correctly applied to clades of organisms, not to individual traits possessed by the organisms--although it can be misused in this manner in technical literature.
Brain damage	Brain damage is the destruction or degeneration of brain cells. Brain injuries occur due to a wide range of internal and external factors. A common category with the greatest number of injuries is traumatic brain injury (TBI) following physical trauma or head injury from an outside source, and the term acquired brain injury (ABI) is used in appropriate circles, to differentiate brain injuries occurring after birth, from injury due to a disorder or congenital malady.
Engram	Engrams are a hypothetical means by which memory traces are stored as biophysical or biochemical changes in the brain (and other neural tissue) in response to external stimuli. They are also sometimes thought of as a neural network or fragment of memory, sometimes using a hologram analogy to describe its action in light of results showing that memory appears not to be localized in the brain. The existence of engrams is posited by some scientific theories to explain the persistence of memory and how memories are stored in the brain.

Hippocampus	The hippocampus is a major component of the brains of humans and other mammals. It belongs to the limbic system and plays important roles in long-term memory and spatial navigation. Like the cerebral cortex, with which it is closely associated, it is a paired structure, with mirror-image halves in the left and right sides of the brain. In humans and other primates, the hippocampus is located inside the medial temporal lobe, beneath the cortical surface. It contains two main interlocking parts: Ammon's horn and the dentate gyrus.
Place cell	Place cells are neurons in the hippocampus that exhibit a high rate of firing whenever an animal is in a specific location in an environment corresponding to the cell's 'place field'. These neurons are distinct from other neurons with spatial firing properties, such as grid cells, border cells, head direction cells, and spatial view cells. In the CA1 and CA3 hippocampal subfields, place cells are believed to be pyramidal cells, while those in the dentate gyrus are believed to be granule cells.
Spatial memory	In cognitive psychology and neuroscience, spatial memory is the part of memory responsible for recording information about one's environment and its spatial orientation. For example, a person's spatial memory is required in order to navigate around a familiar city, just as a rat's spatial memory is needed to learn the location of food at the end of a maze. It is often argued that a person's or animal's spatial memories are summarised in a cognitive map.
Working memory	Working memory has been defined as the system which actively holds information in the mind to do verbal and nonverbal tasks such as reasoning and comprehension, and to make it available for further information processing. Working memory tasks are those that require the goal-oriented active monitoring or manipulation of information or behaviors in the face of interfering processes and distractions. Working memory can only retain a limited amount of information; however, its capacity can be increased by use of a method known as chunking.
Sensory cortex	The sensory cortex can refer informally to the primary somatosensory cortex, on left and right hemisphere): the visual cortex on the occipital lobes, the auditory cortex on the temporal lobes, the primary olfactory cortex on the uncus of the piriform region of the temporal lobes, the gustatory cortex on the insular lobe (also referred to as the insular cortex), and the primary somatosensory cortex on the anterior parietal lobes. Just posterior to the primary somatosensory cortex lies the somatosensory association cortex, which integrates sensory information from the primary somatosensory cortex. to construct an understanding of the object being felt.
Neuroplasticity	Neuroplasticity refers to the susceptibility to physiological changes of the nervous system, due to changes in behavior, environment, neural processes, or parts of the body other than the nervous system. The brain changes throughout life.

Chapter 11. Learning, Memory, and Amnesia

Prefrontal cortex	The prefrontal cortex is the anterior part of the frontal lobes of the brain, lying in front of the motor and premotor areas. This brain region has been implicated in planning complex cognitive behavior, personality expression, decision making and moderating social behavior. The basic activity of this brain region is considered to be orchestration of thoughts and actions in accordance with internal goals.
Long-term potentiation	In neuroscience, long-term potentiation is a long-lasting enhancement in signal transmission between two neurons that results from stimulating them synchronously. It is one of several phenomena underlying synaptic plasticity, the ability of chemical synapses to change their strength. As memories are thought to be encoded by modification of synaptic strength, Long term potentiation is widely considered one of the major cellular mechanisms that underlies learning and memory.
NMDA receptor	The NMDA receptor a glutamate receptor, is the predominant molecular device for controlling synaptic plasticity and memory function. The NMDAR is a specific type of ionotropic glutamate receptor. NMDA (N-methyl-D-aspartate) is the name of a selective agonist that binds to NMDA receptors but not to other glutamate receptors.
Dendritic spine	A dendritic spine is a small membranous protrusion from a neuron's dendrite that typically receives input from a single synapse of an axon. Dendritic spines serve as a storage site for synaptic strength and help transmit electrical signals to the neuron's cell body. Most spines have a bulbous head (the spine head), and a thin neck that connects the head of the spine to the shaft of the dendrite.

1. _____ is the destruction or degeneration of brain cells. Brain injuries occur due to a wide range of internal and external factors. A common category with the greatest number of injuries is traumatic brain injury (TBI) following physical trauma or head injury from an outside source, and the term acquired brain injury (ABI) is used in appropriate circles, to differentiate brain injuries occurring after birth, from injury due to a disorder or congenital malady.

   a. Carl Rogers theory evaluation
   b. Cetancodontamorpha
   c. Cetruminantia
   d. Brain damage

2. . _____ is the recording of electrical activity along the scalp. EEG measures voltage fluctuations resulting from ionic current flows within the neurons of the brain.

In clinical contexts, EEG refers to the recording of the brain's spontaneous electrical activity over a short period of time, usually 20-40 minutes, as recorded from multiple electrodes placed on the scalp.

a. Electroencephalography

b. Imagined speech

c. Informant

d. Adult ADHD Self-Report Scale

3. In neuroscience, _____ is a long-lasting enhancement in signal transmission between two neurons that results from stimulating them synchronously. It is one of several phenomena underlying synaptic plasticity, the ability of chemical synapses to change their strength. As memories are thought to be encoded by modification of synaptic strength, Long term potentiation is widely considered one of the major cellular mechanisms that underlies learning and memory.

a. Mirror neuron

b. Morris water navigation task

c. Long-term potentiation

d. Neuropsychopharmacology

4. _____ has been defined as the system which actively holds information in the mind to do verbal and nonverbal tasks such as reasoning and comprehension, and to make it available for further information processing. _____ tasks are those that require the goal-oriented active monitoring or manipulation of information or behaviors in the face of interfering processes and distractions. _____ can only retain a limited amount of information; however, its capacity can be increased by use of a method known as chunking.

a. Working memory training

b. Working memory

c. Flow

d. 6-3-5 Brainwriting

5. _____ is a neurological disorder caused by the lack of thiamine (vitamin B_1) in the brain. Its onset is linked to chronic alcohol abuse and/or severe malnutrition. The syndrome is named after Sergei Korsakoff, the neuropsychiatrist who popularized the theory.

a. Korsakoff's syndrome

b. Phantom eye syndrome

c. Subclavian steal syndrome

d. myelodysplastic syndrome

1. d
2. a
3. c
4. b
5. a

You can take the complete Chapter Practice Test

for Chapter 11. Learning, Memory, and Amnesia
on all key terms, persons, places, and concepts.

Online 99 Cents

http://www.epub3.10.9241.11.cram101.com/

Use www.Cram101.com for all your study needs

including Cram101's online interactive problem solving labs in

chemistry, statistics, mathematics, and more.

Chapter 12. Hunger, Eating, and Health

Anorexia nervosa

Set point

Starvation

Amnesia

Colon

Glucose

Adipose tissue

Gluconeogenesis

Insulin

Olfaction

Conditioned taste aversion

Taste aversion

Thiamine

Malaise

Classical conditioning

Sensory-specific satiety

Palatability

Ventromedial hypothalamus

Hypothalamus

	Aphagia

	Cholecystokinin

	Serotonin

	Mortality rate

	Basal metabolic rate

	Dexfenfluramine

	Leptin

	Bulimia nervosa

CHAPTER HIGHLIGHTS & NOTES: KEY TERMS, PEOPLE, PLACES, CONCEPTS

Anorexia nervosa	The differential diagnoses of anorexia nervosa (AN) include various medical and psychological conditions which may be misdiagnosed as (AN), in some cases these conditions may be comorbid with anorexia nervosa (AN). The misdiagnosis of AN is not uncommon. In one instance a case of achalasia was misdiagnosed as AN and the patient spent two months confined to a psychiatric hospital.
Set point	In medicine, the term set point refers to any one of a number of quantities (e.g. body weight, body temperature) which the body tries to keep at a particular value. This concept is relevant to practices of physiology and psychology, among others. Example quantities with set points are body weight and happiness, both believed to have values that are difficult to change.
Starvation	Starvation is a severe reduction in vitamin, nutrient and energy intake. It is the most extreme form of malnutrition. In humans, prolonged starvation can cause permanent organ damage and eventually, death.
Amnesia	Amnesia is a condition in which one's memory is lost. The causes of amnesia have traditionally been divided into certain categories.

Chapter 12. Hunger, Eating, and Health

Colon	A colon is a rhetorical figure consisting of a clause which is grammatically, but not logically, complete. In Latin, it is called a membrum or membrum orationis. Sentences consisting of two cola are called dicola; those with three are tricola.
Glucose	Glucose is a simple monosaccharide found in plants. It is one of the three dietary monosaccharides, along with fructose and galactose, that are absorbed directly into the bloodstream during digestion. An important carbohydrate in biology, cells use it as the primary source of energy and a metabolic intermediate.
Adipose tissue	In biology, adipose tissue or body fat or fat depot or just fat is loose connective tissue composed of adipocytes. It is technically composed of roughly only 80% fat; fat in its solitary state exists in the liver and muscles. Adipose tissue is derived from lipoblasts.
Gluconeogenesis	Gluconeogenesis is a metabolic pathway that results in the generation of glucose from non-carbohydrate carbon substrates such as lactate, glycerol, and glucogenic amino acids. It is one of the two main mechanisms humans and many other animals use to keep blood glucose levels from dropping too low (hypoglycemia). The other means of maintaining blood glucose levels is through the degradation of glycogen (glycogenolysis).
Insulin	Insulin is a hormone that is central to regulating carbohydrate and fat metabolism in the body. Insulin causes cells in the liver, muscle, and fat tissue to take up glucose from the blood, storing it as glycogen in the liver and muscle. Insulin stops the use of fat as an energy source by inhibiting the release of glucagon. When insulin is absent, glucose is not taken up by body cells and the body begins to use fat as an energy source or gluconeogenesis; for example, by transfer of lipids from adipose tissue to the liver for mobilization as an energy source. As its level is a central metabolic control mechanism, its status is also used as a control signal to other body systems (such as amino acid uptake by body cells). In addition, it has several other anabolic effects throughout the body.
Olfaction	Olfaction is the sense of smell. This sense is mediated by specialized sensory cells of the nasal cavity of vertebrates, and, by analogy, sensory cells of the antennae of invertebrates. Many vertebrates, including most mammals and reptiles, have two distinct olfactory systems--the main olfactory system, and the accessory olfactory system (mainly used to detect pheremones).
Conditioned taste aversion	Conditioned taste aversion, a term coined by Seligman and Hager, is an example of classical conditioning or Pavlovian conditioning. Conditioned taste aversion occurs when a subject associates the taste of a certain food with symptoms caused by a toxic, spoiled, or poisonous substance.

	Generally, taste aversion is caused after ingestion of the food causes nausea, sickness, or vomiting. The ability to develop a taste aversion is considered an adaptive trait or survival mechanism that trains the body to avoid poisonous substances (e.g., poisonous berries) before they can cause harm.
Taste aversion	Conditioned taste aversion, also known as Garcia effect (after Dr. John Garcia), and as 'Sauce-Bearnaise Syndrome', a term coined by Seligman and Hager, is an example of classical conditioning or Pavlovian conditioning. Conditioned taste aversion occurs when a subject associates the taste of a certain food with symptoms caused by a toxic, spoiled, or poisonous substance. Generally, taste aversion is caused after ingestion of the food causes nausea, sickness, or vomiting.
Thiamine	Thiamine is a water-soluble vitamin of the B complex. First named aneurin for the detrimental neurological effects of its lack in the diet, it was eventually assigned the generic descriptor name vitamin B_1. Its phosphate derivatives are involved in many cellular processes. The best-characterized form is thiamine pyrophosphate (TPP), a coenzyme in the catabolism of sugars and amino acids. In yeast, TPP is also required in the first step of alcoholic fermentation.
Malaise	Malaise is a feeling of general discomfort or uneasiness, of being 'out of sorts', often the first indication of an infection or other disease. Malaise is often defined in medical literature as a 'general feeling of being unwell'. This word is originally a French word existing since the 12th century.
Classical conditioning	Classical conditioning is a form of learning in which the conditioned stimulus or CS, comes to signal the occurrence of a second stimulus, the unconditioned stimulus or US. (A stimulus is a factor that causes a response in an organism). The US is usually a biologically significant stimulus such as food or pain that elicits a response from the start; this is called the unconditioned response or UR. The CS usually produces no particular response at first, but after conditioning it elicits the conditioned response or CR. Classical conditioning differs from operant or instrumental conditioning, in which behavior emitted by the subject is strengthened or weakened by its consequences (i.e. reward or punishment). Conditioning is usually done by pairing the two stimuli, as in Pavlov's classic experiments.
Sensory-specific satiety	Sensory-specific satiety is a sensory hedonic phenomenon that refers to the declining satisfaction generated by the consumption of a certain type of food, and the consequent renewal in appetite resulting from the exposure to a new flavor or food. The phenomenon was first described in 1956 by the French physiologist Jacques Le Magnen. The term has been coined in 1981 by Barbara J. Rolls and Edmund T. Rolls.

Chapter 12. Hunger, Eating, and Health

Palatability	Palatability is the hedonic reward provided by foods or fluids that are agreeable to the 'palate' in regard to the homeostatic satisfaction of nutritional, water, or energy needs. The palatability of a food or fluid, unlike its flavor or taste, varies with the state of an individual: it is lower after consumption and higher when deprived. Palatability of foods, however, can be learned.
Ventromedial hypothalamus	The ventromedial hypothalamus is a distinct morphological nucleus involved in feeding, fear, thermoregulation, and sexual activity.' Division
	It has four subdivisions:•anterior (VMHa)•dorsomedial (VMHdm)•ventrolateral (VMHvl)•central (VMHc)
	These subdivisions differ anatomically, neurochemically, and behaviorally.
	Lateral Hypothalamus: This region of the brain is associated with hunger recognition.
	Ventromedial Hypothalamus: This nuclear region is involved with the recognition of the feeling of fullness.
Hypothalamus	The Hypothalamus is a portion of the brain that contains a number of small nuclei with a variety of functions. One of the most important functions of the hypothalamus is to link the nervous system to the endocrine system via the pituitary gland (hypophysis).
	The hypothalamus is located below the thalamus, just above the brain stem.
Aphagia	Aphagia is the inability or refusal to swallow.' It is related to dysphagia, which is difficulty swallowing, and odynophagia, painful swallowing.
Cholecystokinin	Cholecystokinin is a peptide hormone of the gastrointestinal system responsible for stimulating the digestion of fat and protein. Cholecystokinin, previously called pancreozymin, is synthesised by I-cells in the mucosal epithelium of the small intestine and secreted in the duodenum, the first segment of the small intestine, and causes the release of digestive enzymes and bile from the pancreas and gallbladder, respectively. It also acts as a hunger suppressant.
Serotonin	Serotonin is a monoamine neurotransmitter. Biochemically derived from tryptophan, serotonin is primarily found in the gastrointestinal (GI) tract, platelets, and in the central nervous system (CNS) of animals including humans. It is a well-known contributor to feelings of well-being; therefore it is also known as a 'happiness hormone' despite not being a hormone.
Mortality rate	Mortality rate is a measure of the number of deaths (in general, or due to a specific cause) in some population, scaled to the size of that population, per unit time.

	Mortality rate is typically expressed in units of deaths per 1000 individuals per year; thus, a mortality rate of 9.5 in a population of 100,000 would mean 950 deaths per year in that entire population, or 0.95% out of the total. It is distinct from morbidity rate, which refers to the number of individuals in poor health during a given time period (the prevalence rate) or the number of newly appearing cases of the disease per unit of time (incidence rate).
Basal metabolic rate	Basal Metabolic Rate and the closely related resting metabolic rate (RMR), is the amount of daily energy expended by animals at rest. Rest is defined as existing in a neutrally temperate environment while in the post-absorptive state. In plants, different considerations apply.
Dexfenfluramine	Dexfenfluramine, marketed as dexfenfluramine hydrochloride under the name Redux, is a serotoninergic anorectic drug: it reduces appetite by increasing the amount of extracellular serotonin in the brain. It is the d-enantiomer of fenfluramine and is structurally similar to amphetamine, but lacks any psychologically stimulating effects. Dexfenfluramine was for some years in the mid-1990s approved by the United States Food and Drug Administration for the purposes of weight loss.
Leptin	Leptin is a 16-kDa protein hormone that plays a key role in regulating energy intake and energy expenditure, including appetite/hunger and metabolism. It is one of the most important adipose-derived hormones. The Ob(Lep) gene (Ob for obese, Lep for leptin) is located on chromosome 7 in humans.
Bulimia nervosa	Bulimia nervosa is an eating disorder characterized by restraining of food intake for a period of time followed by an over intake or binging period that results in feelings of guilt and low self-esteem. The median age of onset is 18. Sufferers attempt to overcome these feelings in a number of ways. The most common form is defensive vomiting, sometimes called purging; fasting, the use of laxatives, enemas, diuretics, and over exercising are also common.

Chapter 12. Hunger, Eating, and Health

1. In medicine, the term _____ refers to any one of a number of quantities (e.g. body weight, body temperature) which the body tries to keep at a particular value. This concept is relevant to practices of physiology and psychology, among others. Example quantities with _____s are body weight and happiness, both believed to have values that are difficult to change.

   a. Social experiment
   b. Set point
   c. Spillover-crossover model
   d. Stimulus control

2. _____ is a metabolic pathway that results in the generation of glucose from non-carbohydrate carbon substrates such as lactate, glycerol, and glucogenic amino acids.

   It is one of the two main mechanisms humans and many other animals use to keep blood glucose levels from dropping too low (hypoglycemia). The other means of maintaining blood glucose levels is through the degradation of glycogen (glycogenolysis).

   a. Carl Rogers theory evaluation
   b. Gluconeogenesis
   c. Consolatio
   d. Contrast

3. The differential diagnoses of _____ (AN) include various medical and psychological conditions which may be misdiagnosed as (AN), in some cases these conditions may be comorbid with _____ (AN). The misdiagnosis of AN is not uncommon. In one instance a case of achalasia was misdiagnosed as AN and the patient spent two months confined to a psychiatric hospital.

   a. Organized Crime Control Act
   b. Anorexia nervosa
   c. Uniform Determination of Death Act
   d. Aeron chair

4. _____ is the inability or refusal to swallow.' It is related to dysphagia, which is difficulty swallowing, and odynophagia, painful swallowing.

   a. Ileum
   b. Anal canal
   c. Aphagia
   d. Supraoptic nucleus

5. . _____ is a severe reduction in vitamin, nutrient and energy intake. It is the most extreme form of malnutrition. In humans, prolonged _____ can cause permanent organ damage and eventually, death.

   a. Sudden infant death syndrome

b. Systemic inflammatory response syndrome

c. Terminal dehydration

d. Starvation

1. b
2. b
3. b
4. c
5. d

You can take the complete Chapter Practice Test

for Chapter 12. Hunger, Eating, and Health
on all key terms, persons, places, and concepts.

Online 99 Cents

http://www.epub3.10.9241.12.cram101.com/

Use www.Cram101.com for all your study needs

including Cram101's online interactive problem solving labs in

chemistry, statistics, mathematics, and more.

Chapter 13. Hormones and Sex

CHAPTER OUTLINE: KEY TERMS, PEOPLE, PLACES, CONCEPTS

_____ | Endocrine glands

_____ | Hormone

_____ | Neuroendocrinology

_____ | Steroid

_____ | Adrenal glands

_____ | Gamete

_____ | Gonad

_____ | Hypothalamus

_____ | Pineal gland

_____ | Pituitary gland

_____ | Sexual intercourse

_____ | X chromosome

_____ | Zygote

_____ | Adrenal cortex

_____ | Anterior pituitary

_____ | Estradiol

_____ | Estrogen

_____ | Glucose

_____ | Gonadotropin

Progestin

Testosterone

Neuroendocrine cell

Oxytocin

Vasopressin

Releasing hormone

Thyroid-stimulating hormone

Thyrotropin-releasing hormone

Gonadotropin-releasing hormone

Luteinizing hormone

Cerebral cortex

Sexual differentiation

Glans

Clitoral hood

Dihydrotestosterone

Defeminization

Feminization

Adrenocorticotropic hormone

Growth hormone

Chapter 13. Hormones and Sex

CHAPTER OUTLINE: KEY TERMS, PEOPLE, PLACES, CONCEPTS

Puberty

Secondary sex characteristic

Injection

Congenital adrenal hyperplasia

Cortisol

Mutation

Sexual identity

Mastectomy

Anabolic steroid

Estrous cycle

Fertility

Progesterone

Amenorrhoea

Cerebral hypoxia

Testicular atrophy

Sexually dimorphic nucleus

Dopamine

Periaqueductal gray

Sexual orientation

	Transsexualism

Endocrine glands	Endocrine glands are glands of the endocrine system that secrete their products, hormones, directly into the blood rather than through a duct. The main endocrine glands include the pituitary gland, pancreas, ovaries, testes, thyroid gland, and adrenal glands. The hypothalamus is a neuroendocrine organ.
Hormone	A hormone is a chemical released by a cell or a gland in one part of the body that sends out messages that affect cells in other parts of the organism. Only a small amount of hormone is required to alter cell metabolism. In essence, it is a chemical messenger that transports a signal from one cell to another. All multicellular organisms produce hormones; plant hormones are also called phytohormones. Hormones in animals are often transported in the blood. Cells respond to a hormone when they express a specific receptor for that hormone. The hormone binds to the receptor protein, resulting in the activation of a signal transduction mechanism that ultimately leads to cell type-specific responses.
Neuroendocrinology	Neuroendocrinology is the study of the extensive interactions between the nervous system and the endocrine system, including the biological features of the cells that participate, and how they functionally communicate. The nervous and endocrine systems often act together to regulate the physiological processes of the human body. Neuroendocrinology arose from the recognition that the brain, especially the hypothalamus, controls secretion of pituitary gland hormones, and has subsequently expanded to investigate numerous interconnections of the endocrine and nervous systems.
Steroid	A steroid is a type of organic compound that contains a characteristic arrangement of four cycloalkane rings that are joined to each other. Examples of steroids include the dietary fat cholesterol, the sex hormones estradiol and testosterone, and the anti-inflammatory drug dexamethasone. The core of steroids is composed of twenty carbon atoms bonded together that take the form of four fused rings: three cyclohexane rings and one cyclopentane ring (the D ring).

Adrenal glands	In mammals, the adrenal glands are endocrine glands that sit at the top of the kidneys; in humans, the right adrenal gland is triangular shaped, while the left adrenal gland is semilunar shaped. They are chiefly responsible for releasing hormones in response to stress through the synthesis of corticosteroids such as cortisol and catecholamines such as epinephrine (adrenaline) and norepinephrine. They also produce androgens.
Gamete	A gamete is a cell that fuses with another cell during fertilization (conception) in organisms that reproduce sexually. In species that produce two morphologically distinct types of gametes, and in which each individual produces only one type, a female is any individual that produces the larger type of gamete--called an ovum (or egg)--and a male produces the smaller tadpole-like type--called a sperm. This is an example of anisogamy or heterogamy, the condition wherein females and males produce gametes of different sizes (this is the case in humans; the human ovum is approximately 20 times larger than the human sperm cell).
Gonad	The gonad is the organ that makes gametes. The gonads in males are the testicles and the gonads in females are the ovaries. The product, gametes, are haploid germ cells.
Hypothalamus	The Hypothalamus is a portion of the brain that contains a number of small nuclei with a variety of functions. One of the most important functions of the hypothalamus is to link the nervous system to the endocrine system via the pituitary gland (hypophysis). The hypothalamus is located below the thalamus, just above the brain stem.
Pineal gland	The pineal gland is a small endocrine gland in the vertebrate brain. It produces the serotonin derivative melatonin, a hormone that affects the modulation of wake/sleep patterns and seasonal functions. Its shape resembles a tiny pine cone (hence its name), and it is located near the center of the brain, between the two hemispheres, tucked in a groove where the two rounded thalamic bodies join.
Pituitary gland	In vertebrate anatomy the pituitary gland, is an endocrine gland about the size of a pea and weighing 0.5 g (0.02 oz)., in humans. It is a protrusion off the bottom of the hypothalamus at the base of the brain, and rests in a small, bony cavity (sella turcica) covered by a dural fold (diaphragma sellae). The pituitary is functionally connected to the hypothalamus by the median eminence via a small tube called the infundibular stem (Pituitary Stalk).
Sexual intercourse	Sexual intercourse, commonly refers to the act in which the male reproductive organ enters the female reproductive tract. The two entities may be of opposite sexes, or they may be hermaphroditic, as is the case with snails.

Chapter 13. Hormones and Sex

X chromosome	The X chromosome is one of the two sex-determining chromosomes in many animal species, including mammals (the other is the Y chromosome). It is a part of the XY sex-determination system and X0 sex-determination system. The X chromosome was named for its unique properties by early researchers, which resulted in the naming of its counterpart Y chromosome, for the next letter in the alphabet, after it was discovered later.
Zygote	A zygote is the initial cell formed when a new organism is produced by means of sexual reproduction. A zygote is synthesized from the union of two gametes, and constitutes the first stage in a unique organism's development. Zygotes are usually produced by a fertilization event between two haploid cells--an ovum from a female and a sperm cell from a male--which combine to form the single diploid cell.
Adrenal cortex	Situated along the perimeter of the adrenal gland, the adrenal cortex mediates the stress response through the production of mineralocorticoids and glucocorticoids, including aldosterone and cortisol respectively. It is also a secondary site of androgen synthesis.
Anterior pituitary	A major organ of the endocrine system, the anterior pituitary is the glandular, anterior lobe of the pituitary gland. The anterior pituitary regulates several physiological processes including stress, growth, and reproduction. Its regulatory functions are achieved through the secretion of various peptide hormones that act on target organs including the adrenal gland, liver, bone, thyroid gland, and gonads.
Estradiol	Estradiol is a sex hormone. Estradiol is the predominant sex hormone present in females. It is also present in males, being produced as an active metabolic product of testosterone. It represents the major estrogen in humans. Estradiol has not only a critical impact on reproductive and sexual functioning, but also affects other organs including the bones.
Estrogen	Estrogens (AmE), oestrogens , are a group of compounds named for their importance in the estrous cycle of humans and other animals, and functioning as the primary female sex hormones. Natural estrogens are steroid hormones, while some synthetic ones are non-steroidal.
Glucose	Glucose is a simple monosaccharide found in plants. It is one of the three dietary monosaccharides, along with fructose and galactose, that are absorbed directly into the bloodstream during digestion. An important carbohydrate in biology, cells use it as the primary source of energy and a metabolic intermediate.
Gonadotropin	Glycoprotein hormone

	Gonadotropins are protein hormones secreted by gonadotrope cells of the pituitary gland of vertebrates. This is a family of proteins, which include the mammalian hormones follitropin (FSH), lutropin (LH), placental chorionic gonadotropins hCG and eCG and chorionic gonadotropin as well as at least two forms of fish gonadotropins. These hormones are central to the complex endocrine system that regulates normal growth, sexual development, and reproductive function.
Progestin	A progestin is a synthetic progestogen that has progestinic effects similar to progesterone. The two most common uses of progestins are for hormonal contraception (either alone or with an estrogen), and to prevent endometrial hyperplasia from unopposed estrogen in hormone replacement therapy. Progestins are also used to treat secondary amenorrhea, dysfunctional uterine bleeding and endometriosis, and as palliative treatment of endometrial cancer, renal cell carcinoma, breast cancer, and prostate cancer.
Testosterone	Testosterone is a steroid hormone from the androgen group and is found in mammals, reptiles, birds, and other vertebrates. In mammals, testosterone is primarily secreted in the testes of males and the ovaries of females, although small amounts are also secreted by the adrenal glands. It is the principal male sex hormone and an anabolic steroid.
Neuroendocrine cell	Neuroendocrine cells (neurosecretory cells) are cells that receive neuronal input (neurotransmitters released by nerve cells) and, as a consequence of this input, release message molecules (hormones) to the blood. In this way they bring about an integration between the nervous system and the endocrine system, a process known as neuroendocrine integration. An example of a neuroendocrine cell is the cell of the adrenal medulla (innermost part of the adrenal gland) which releases adrenalin to the blood.
Oxytocin	Oxytocin ( ) is a mammalian hormone that acts primarily as a neuromodulator in the brain.
	Oxytocin is best known for its roles in sexual reproduction, in particular during and after childbirth. It is released in large amounts after distension of the cervix and uterus during labor, facilitating birth, and after stimulation of the nipples, facilitating breastfeeding.
Vasopressin	Arginine vasopressin also known as vasopressin, argipressin or antidiuretic hormone (ADH), is a neurohypophysial hormone found in most mammals. Vasopressin is responsible for increasing water absorption in the collecting ducts of the kidney nephron. Vasopressin increases water permeability of kidney collecting duct by inducing translocation of aquaporin-CD water channels in the kidney nephron collecting duct plasma membrane.
Releasing hormone	A releasing hormone is a hormone whose main purpose is to control the release of another hormone.

Chapter 13. Hormones and Sex

Thyroid-stimulating hormone	Thyroid-stimulating hormone is a peptide hormone synthesized and secreted by thyrotrope cells in the anterior pituitary gland, which regulates the endocrine function of the thyroid gland. Thyroid stimulating hormone stimulates the thyroid gland to secrete the hormones thyroxine (T_4) and triiodothyronine (T_3). Thyroid stimulating hormone production is controlled by thyrotropin-releasing hormone (TRH), which is manufactured in the hypothalamus and transported to the anterior pituitary gland via the superior hypophyseal artery, where it increases Thyroid stimulating hormone production and release.
Thyrotropin-releasing hormone	Thyrotropin-releasing hormone is a tropic, tripeptidal hormone that stimulates the release of TSH and prolactin from the anterior pituitary. Thyrotropin releasing hormone has been used clinically for the treatment of spinocerebellar degeneration and disturbance of consciousness in humans. Synthesis Thyrotropin releasing hormone is produced by the hypothalamus in medial neurons of the paraventricular nucleus.
Gonadotropin-releasing hormone	Gonadotropin-releasing hormone also known as Luteinizing-hormone-releasing hormone (LHRH) and luliberin, is a tropic peptide hormone responsible for the release of follicle-stimulating hormone (FSH) and luteinizing hormone (LH) from the anterior pituitary. GnRH is synthesized and released from neurons within the hypothalamus. The peptide belongs to gonadotropin-releasing hormone family.
Luteinizing hormone	Luteinizing hormone is a hormone produced by the anterior pituitary gland. In females, an acute rise of luteinizing hormone called the luteinizing hormone surge triggers ovulation and development of the corpus luteum. In males, where luteinizing hormone had also been called interstitial cell-stimulating hormone (ICSH), it stimulates Leydig cell production of testosterone.
Cerebral cortex	The cerebral cortex is a sheet of neural tissue that is outermost to the cerebrum of the mammalian brain. It plays a key role in memory, attention, perceptual awareness, thought, language, and consciousness. It is constituted of up to six horizontal layers, each of which has a different composition in terms of neurons and connectivity.
Sexual differentiation	Sexual differentiation is the process of development of the differences between males and females from an undifferentiated zygote (fertilized egg). As male and female individuals develop from zygotes into fetuses, into infants, children, adolescents, and eventually into adults, sex and gender differences at many levels develop: genes, chromosomes, gonads, hormones, anatomy, and psyche. Sex differences range from nearly absolute to simply statistical.

Glans	The glans is a vascular structure located at the tip of the penis in men or a homologous genital structure of the clitoris in women. Structure The exterior structure of the glans consists of mucous membrane, which is usually covered by foreskin or clitoral hood in naturally developed genitalia. This covering, called the prepuce, is normally retractable in adulthood.
Clitoral hood	In female human anatomy, the clitoral hood, (also called preputium clitoridis and clitoral prepuce), is a fold of skin that surrounds and protects the clitoral glans. It develops as part of the labia minora and is homologous with the foreskin (equally called prepuce) in male genitals. Variation This is a protective hood of skin that covers the clitoral glans.
Dihydrotestosterone	Dihydrotestosterone or 5α-dihydrotestosterone also known as androstanolone (5α-androstan-17β-ol-3-one) as well as 17β-hydroxy-5α-androstan-3-one, is a sex steroid and androgen hormone. The enzyme 5α-reductase synthesizes DHT in the prostate, testes, hair follicles, and adrenal glands. This enzyme reduces the 4,5 double-bond of the hormone testosterone.
Defeminization	Defeminization is a term in developmental biology, especially zoology, referring to an aspect of the process of sexual differentiation by which a potential female-specific structure, function, or behavior is prevented from developing by one of the processes of male development. Although the term might seem to imply 'removal' of female characteristics, in nearly all biological contexts it refers to prevention of an aspect of female development from manifesting. In human biology of gender, the best known example of this is the prevention of development of the müllerian duct derivatives by anti-müllerian hormone (AMH) in the 3rd and 4th months of fetal development, though the term is not commonly used in discussions of human development.
Feminization	In biology and medicine, feminization refers to the development in an organism of physical or behavioral characteristics unique to the female of the species. This may represent a normal developmental process, contributing to sexual differentiation. Feminization can also be induced by environmental factors, and this phenomenon has been observed in several animal species.
Adrenocorticotropic hormone	Adrenocorticotropic hormone also known as corticotropin, is a polypeptide tropic hormone produced and secreted by the anterior pituitary gland.

Chapter 13. Hormones and Sex

	It is an important component of the hypothalamic-pituitary-adrenal axis and is often produced in response to biological stress (along with its precursor corticotropin-releasing hormone from the hypothalamus). Its principal effects are increased production and release of corticosteroids.
Growth hormone	Growth hormone is a protein-based peptide hormone. It stimulates growth, cell reproduction and regeneration in humans and other animals. Growth hormone is a 191-amino acid, single-chain polypeptide that is synthesized, stored, and secreted by the somatotroph cells within the lateral wings of the anterior pituitary gland.
Puberty	Puberty is the process of physical changes by which a child's body becomes an adult body capable of reproduction. Puberty is initiated by hormone signals from the brain to the gonads (the ovaries and testes). In response, the gonads produce a variety of hormones that stimulate the growth, function, or transformation of brain, bones, muscle, blood, skin, hair, breasts, and sex organs.
Secondary sex characteristic	Secondary sex characteristics are features that distinguish the two sexes of a species, but that are not directly part of the reproductive system. They are believed to be the product of sexual selection for traits which give an individual an advantage over its rivals in courtship and aggressive interactions. They are distinguished from the primary sex characteristics: the sex organs, which are directly necessary for reproduction to occur.
Injection	An injection (often referred to as a 'shot' or a 'jab') is an infusion method of putting fluid into the body, usually with a hollow needle and a syringe which is pierced through the skin to a sufficient depth for the material to be forced into the body. An injection follows a parenteral route of administration; that is, administered other than through the digestive tract.
	There are several methods of injection or infusion, including intradermal, subcutaneous, intramuscular, intravenous, intraosseous, and intraperitoneal.
Congenital adrenal hyperplasia	Congenital adrenal hyperplasia refers to any of several autosomal recessive diseases resulting from mutations of genes for enzymes mediating the biochemical steps of production of cortisol from cholesterol by the adrenal glands (steroidogenesis). Most of these conditions involve excessive or deficient production of sex steroids and can alter development of primary or secondary sex characteristics in some affected infants, children, or adults. Congenital adrenal hyperplasia is one of the possible underlying synthesis problems in Addison's disease.
Cortisol	Cortisol is a steroid hormone, or glucocorticoid, produced by the adrenal gland. It is released in response to stress and a low level of blood glucocorticoids. Its primary functions are to increase blood sugar through gluconeogenesis; suppress the immune system; and aid in fat, protein and carbohydrate metabolism.

Mutation	In molecular biology and genetics, mutations are changes in a genomic sequence: the DNA sequence of a cell's genome or the DNA or RNA sequence of a virus. These random sequences can be defined as sudden and spontaneous changes in the cell. Mutations are caused by radiation, viruses, transposons and mutagenic chemicals, as well as errors that occur during meiosis or DNA replication.
Sexual identity	Sexual identity refers to how one thinks of oneself in terms of whom one is sexually and romantically attracted to. Sexual identity and sexual behavior are closely related to sexual orientation, but they are distinguished, with identity referring to an individual's conception of themselves, behavior referring to actual sexual acts performed by the individual, and orientation referring to 'fantasies, attachments and longings.' Sexual identity may or may not relate to their actual sexual orientation. In a 1990 study by the Social Organization of Sexuality, only 16% of women and 36% of men who reported some level of same-sex attraction had a homosexual or bisexual identity.
Mastectomy	In medicine, mastectomy is the medical term for the surgical removal of one or both breasts, partially or completely. Mastectomy is usually done to treat breast cancer; in some cases, women and some men believed to be at high risk of breast cancer have the operation prophylactically, that is, to prevent cancer rather than treat it. It is also the medical procedure carried out to remove breast cancer tissue in males.
Anabolic steroid	Anabolic steroids, technically known as anabolic-androgen steroids, are drugs which mimic the effects of the male sex hormones testosterone and dihydrotestosterone. They increase protein synthesis within cells, which results in the buildup of cellular tissue (anabolism), especially in muscles. Anabolic steroids also have androgenic and virilizing properties, including the development and maintenance of masculine characteristics such as the growth of the vocal cords and body hair.
Estrous cycle	The estrous cycle comprises the recurring physiologic changes that are induced by reproductive hormones in most mammalian therian females. Estrous cycles start after puberty in sexually mature females and are interrupted by anestrous phases or pregnancies. Typically estrous cycles continue until death.
Fertility	Fertility is the natural capability of giving life. As a measure, 'fertility rate' is the number of children born per couple, person or population. Fertility differs from fecundity, which is defined as the potential for reproduction (influenced by gamete production, fertilisation and carrying a pregnancy to term).

Chapter 13. Hormones and Sex

Progesterone	Progesterone also known as P4 (pregn-4-ene-3,20-dione) is a C-21 steroid hormone involved in the female menstrual cycle, pregnancy (supports gestation) and embryogenesis of humans and other species. Progesterone belongs to a class of hormones called progestogens, and is the major naturally occurring human progestogen. Progesterone was independently discovered by four research groups.
Amenorrhoea	Amenorrhoea amenorrhea (AmE), or amenorrha, is the absence of a menstrual period in a woman of reproductive age. Physiological states of amenorrhoea are seen during pregnancy and lactation (breastfeeding), the latter also forming the basis of a form of contraception known as the lactational amenorrhoea method. Outside of the reproductive years there is absence of menses during childhood and after menopause.
Cerebral hypoxia	Cerebral hypoxia refers to a reduced supply of oxygen to the brain. Cerebral anoxia refers to a complete lack of oxygen to the brain. There are four categories of cerebral hypoxia; in order of severity they are; diffuse cerebral hypoxia focal cerebral ischemia, cerebral infarction, and global cerebral ischemia.
Testicular atrophy	Testicular atrophy is a medical condition in which the male reproductive organs (the testes, which in humans are located in the scrotum) diminish in size and may be accompanied by loss of function. This does not refer to temporary changes, such as those brought on by cold. Some medications can cause testicular atrophy. Anabolic-Androgenic Steroids (AAS) can cause testicular atrophy by reducing the amount of luteinizing hormone (LH) produced by the pituitary gland.
Sexually dimorphic nucleus	Sexually dimorphic nucleus is believed to be related to sexual behavior in animals. It is a cluster of cells located in the preoptic area of hypothalamus of the brain. The volume of Sexually dimorphic nucleus is significantly larger (about twice) in males than in females, caused mainly by greater cell number and larger cell size, in male Sexually dimorphic nucleus. Sexually dimorphic nucleus and its homologues widely exist in human, mammal and some other animal brains, including the third interstitial nucleus of the anterior hypothalamus (INAH3) in humans, ovine sexually dimorphic nucleus in the medial preoptic area/anterior hypothalamus (MPOA/AH) in sheep, sexually dimorphic nucleus in the preoptic area (Sexually dimorphic nucleus-POA) in rats, anterior hypothalamic nucleus (AHdc) in macaques, specific area in medial preoptic nucleus (POM) in quails, etc.
Dopamine	Dopamine, a simple organic chemical in the catecholamine family, plays a number of important physiological roles in the bodies of animals. Its name derives from its chemical structure, which consists of an amine group (NH_2) linked to a catechol structure called dihydroxyphenethylamine, the decarboxyalted form of dihydroxyphenylalanine (acronym DOPA).

Chapter 13. Hormones and Sex

Periaqueductal gray	Periaqueductal gray is the gray matter located around the cerebral aqueduct within the tegmentum of the midbrain. It plays a role in the descending modulation of pain and in defensive behaviour. The ascending pain and temperature fibers of the spinothalamic tract also send information to the PAG via the spinomesencephalic tract .
Sexual orientation	Sexual orientation is an enduring personal quality that inclines people to feel romantic or sexual attraction to persons of the opposite sex or gender, the same sex or gender, or to both sexes or more than one gender. These attractions are generally subsumed under heterosexuality, homosexuality, and bisexuality, while asexuality (the lack of romantic or sexual attraction to others) is sometimes identified as the fourth category. These categories are aspects of the more nuanced nature of sexual identity.
Transsexualism	Transsexualism is an individual's identification with a gender inconsistent or not culturally associated with their assigned sex. Simply put, it defines a person whose assigned sex at birth conflicts with their psychological gender. A medical diagnosis can be made if a person experiences discomfort as a result of a desire to be a member of the opposite sex, or if a person experiences impaired functioning or distress as a result of that gender identification.

1. The _____ is one of the two sex-determining chromosomes in many animal species, including mammals (the other is the Y chromosome). It is a part of the XY sex-determination system and X0 sex-determination system. The _____ was named for its unique properties by early researchers, which resulted in the naming of its counterpart Y chromosome, for the next letter in the alphabet, after it was discovered later.

   a. Carl Rogers theory evaluation
   b. X chromosome
   c. Pegging
   d. Car sex

2. _____ are glands of the endocrine system that secrete their products, hormones, directly into the blood rather than through a duct. The main _____ include the pituitary gland, pancreas, ovaries, testes, thyroid gland, and adrenal glands. The hypothalamus is a neuroendocrine organ.

   a. Endocrine glands
   b. massed learning
   c. Posse Comitatus Act
   d. Wilkinson v Downton

Chapter 13. Hormones and Sex

3. A _____ is a chemical released by a cell or a gland in one part of the body that sends out messages that affect cells in other parts of the organism. Only a small amount of _____ is required to alter cell metabolism. In essence, it is a chemical messenger that transports a signal from one cell to another. All multicellular organisms produce _____s; plant _____s are also called phyto_____s. _____s in animals are often transported in the blood. Cells respond to a _____ when they express a specific receptor for that _____. The _____ binds to the receptor protein, resulting in the activation of a signal transduction mechanism that ultimately leads to cell type-specific responses.

    a. clerk
    b. Homonym
    c. Thorax
    d. Hormone

4. In mammals, the _____ are endocrine glands that sit at the top of the kidneys; in humans, the right _____(s) is triangular shaped, while the left _____(s) is semilunar shaped. They are chiefly responsible for releasing hormones in response to stress through the synthesis of corticosteroids such as cortisol and catecholamines such as epinephrine (adrenaline) and norepinephrine. They also produce androgens.

    a. massed learning
    b. Subfornical organ
    c. Adrenal glands
    d. Chromium

5. _____, a simple organic chemical in the catecholamine family, plays a number of important physiological roles in the bodies of animals. Its name derives from its chemical structure, which consists of an amine group (NH_2) linked to a catechol structure called dihydroxyphenethylamine, the decarboxyalted form of dihydroxyphenylalanine (acronym DOPA). In the brain, _____ functions as a neurotransmitter--a chemical released by nerve cells to send signals to other nerve cells.

    a. Dopaminergic
    b. Dopamine
    c. False neurotransmitter
    d. FMRFamide

1. b
2. a
3. d
4. c
5. b

You can take the complete Chapter Practice Test

for Chapter 13. Hormones and Sex
on all key terms, persons, places, and concepts.

Online 99 Cents

http://www.epub3.10.9241.13.cram101.com/

Use www.Cram101.com for all your study needs

including Cram101's online interactive problem solving labs in

chemistry, statistics, mathematics, and more.

	Delta wave

	Electromyography

	Electrooculography

	Sleep spindle

	REM sleep

	Slow-wave sleep

	Sleepwalking

	Circadian rhythm

	Circadian clock

	Entrainment

	Jet lag

	Microsleep

	Sleep deprivation

	REM rebound

	Antidepressant

	Tricyclic antidepressant

	Encephalitis lethargica

	Reticular activating system

	Optic chiasm

Optic nerve

Optic tract

Retinohypothalamic tract

Melanopsin

Retinal ganglion cell

5-Hydroxytryptophan

Benzodiazepine

Hypnotic drugs

Insomnia

Pineal gland

Raphe nuclei

Stimulant

Anxiety

Hypersomnia

Melatonin

Anxiolytic

Drug tolerance

Narcolepsy

Sleep apnea

	Castration
	Hallucination
	Orexin
	Sleep paralysis
	Sleep inertia
	Mortality rate

CHAPTER HIGHLIGHTS & NOTES: KEY TERMS, PEOPLE, PLACES, CONCEPTS

Delta wave	A delta wave is a high amplitude brain wave with a frequency of oscillation between 0-4 hertz. Delta waves, like other brain waves, are recorded with an electroencephalogram (EEG) and are usually associated with the deepest stages of sleep (3 and 4 NREM), also known as slow-wave sleep (SWS), and aid in characterizing the depth of sleep.
Electromyography	Electromyography is a technique for evaluating and recording the electrical activity produced by skeletal muscles. EMG is performed using an instrument called an electromyograph, to produce a record called an electromyogram. An electromyograph detects the electrical potential generated by muscle cells when these cells are electrically or neurologically activated.
Electrooculography	Electrooculography. is a technique for measuring the resting potential of the retina. The resulting signal is called the electrooculogram.
Sleep spindle	A sleep spindle is a burst of oscillatory brain activity visible on an EEG that occurs during stage 2 sleep. It consists of 12-14 Hz waves that occur for at least 0.5 seconds. Sleep spindles (sometimes referred to as 'sigma bands' or 'sigma waves') may represent periods where the brain is inhibiting processing to keep the sleeper in a tranquil state.
REM sleep	Rapid eye movement sleep (REM sleep) is a normal stage of sleep characterized by the rapid and random movement of the eyes.

Chapter 14. Sleep, Dreaming, and Circadian Rhythms

REM sleep is classified into two categories: tonic and phasic. It was identified and defined by Nathaniel Kleitman, Eugene Aserinsky, and Jon Birtwell in the early 1950s.

Slow-wave sleep	Slow-wave sleep often referred to as deep sleep, consists of stages 3 and 4 of non-rapid eye movement sleep, according to the Rechtschaffen & Kales (R & K) standard of 1968. As of 2008, the American Academy of Sleep Medicine (AASM) has discontinued the use of stage 4, such that the previous stages 3 and 4 now are combined as stage 3. An epoch (30 seconds of sleep) which consists of 20% or more slow wave (delta) sleep, now is considered to be stage 3. The highest arousal thresholds (i.e. difficulty of awakening, such as by a sound of a particular volume) are observed in deep sleep. A person will typically feel more groggy when awoken from slow-wave sleep, and indeed, cognitive tests administered after awakening then indicate that mental performance is somewhat impaired for periods of up to 30 minutes or so, relative to awakenings from other stages.
Sleepwalking	Sleepwalking, is a sleep disorder belonging to the parasomnia family. Sleepwalkers arise from the slow wave sleep stage in a state of low consciousness and perform activities that are usually performed during a state of full consciousness. These activities can be as benign as sitting up in bed, walking to the bathroom, and cleaning, or as hazardous as cooking, driving, having sex, violent gestures, grabbing at hallucinated objects, or even homicide.
Circadian rhythm	A circadian rhythm is an endogenously driven roughly 24-hour cycle in biochemical, physiological, or behavioural processes. Circadian rhythms have been widely observed, in plants, animals, fungi and cyanobacteria . The term 'circadian' comes from the Latin circa, meaning 'around', and diem or dies, meaning 'day'.
Circadian clock	A circadian clock, is a biochemical mechanism that oscillates with a period of 24 hours and is coordinated with the day-night cycle. Circadian clocks are the central mechanisms which drive circadian rhythms. They consist of three major components:•A central oscillator with a period of about 24 hours that keeps time•A series of input pathways to this central oscillator to allow entrainment of the clock•A series of output pathways tied to distinct phases of the oscillator that regulate overt rhythms in biochemistry, physiology, and behavior throughout the organism The clock is reset as the environment changes through an organism's ability to sense external time cues of which the primary one is light.
Entrainment	Entrainment has been used to refer to the process of mode locking of coupled driven oscillators, which is the process whereby two interacting oscillating systems, which have different periods when they function independently, assume a common period. The two oscillators may fall into synchrony, but other phase relationships are also possible.

Jet lag	Jet lag, medically referred to as desynchronosis, is a physiological condition which results from alterations to the body's circadian rhythms; it is classified as one of the circadian rhythm sleep disorders. Jet lag results from rapid long-distance transmeridian (east-west or west-east) travel, as on a jet plane. The condition of jet lag may last several days, and a recovery rate of one day per time zone crossed is a fair guideline.
Microsleep	A microsleep is an episode of sleep which may last for a fraction of a second or up to thirty seconds. Often, it is the result of sleep deprivation, mental fatigue, depression, sleep apnea, hypoxia, narcolepsy, or hypersomnia. For the sleep-deprived, microsleeping can occur at any time, typically without substantial warning.
Sleep deprivation	Sleep deprivation is the condition of not having enough sleep; it can be either chronic or acute. A chronic sleep-restricted state can cause fatigue, daytime sleepiness, clumsiness and weight loss or weight gain. It adversely affects the brain and cognitive function.
REM rebound	REM rebound is the lengthening and increasing frequency and depth of REM sleep which occurs after periods of sleep deprivation. When people are prevented from experiencing REM, they take less time than usual to attain the REM state. Common to those who take certain sleeping aids, it is also often seen in the first few nights after patients with obstructive sleep apnea syndrome are placed on CPAP.
Antidepressant	Antidepressants, are drugs for the treatment of depression. Despite their name, they are often used to treat other conditions, on- or off-label, for conditions such as anxiety disorders, obsessive compulsive disorder, eating disorders, chronic pain, and some hormone-mediated disorders such as dysmenorrhea, and for snoring, migraines, attention-deficit hyperactivity disorder, (ADHD) substance abuse and occasionally even insomnia. Antidepressants are used either alone or combination with other medications.
Tricyclic antidepressant	Tricyclic antidepressants (TCAs) are heterocyclic chemical compounds used primarily as antidepressants. heir chemical structure, which contains three rings of atoms. The tetracyclic antidepressants (TeCAs), which contain four rings of atoms, are a closely related group of antidepressant compounds.
Encephalitis lethargica	Encephalitis lethargica is an atypical form of encephalitis. Also known as 'sleepy sickness' (though different from the sleeping sickness transmitted by the tsetse fly), it was first described by the neurologist Constantin von Economo in 1917. The disease attacks the brain, leaving some victims in a statue-like condition, speechless and motionless.

Chapter 14. Sleep, Dreaming, and Circadian Rhythms

Reticular activating system	The reticular activating system is an area of the brain (including the reticular formation and its connections) responsible for regulating arousal and sleep-wake transitions.
Optic chiasm	The optic chiasm is the part of the brain where the optic nerves (CN II) partially cross. The optic chiasm is located at the bottom of the brain immediately below the hypothalamus. The images on the nasal sides of each retina cross over to the opposite side of the brain via the optic nerve at the optic chiasm.
Optic nerve	The optic nerve, transmits visual information from the retina to the brain. Derived from the embryonic retinal ganglion cell, a diverticulum located in the diencephalon, the optic nerve does not regenerate after transection. The optic nerve is the second of twelve paired cranial nerves but is considered to be part of the central nervous system, as it is derived from an outpouching of the diencephalon during embryonic development.
Optic tract	The optic tract is a part of the visual system in the brain. It is a continuation of the optic nerve and runs from the optic chiasm (where half of the information from each eye crosses sides, and half stays on the same side) to the lateral geniculate nucleus. Right vs. left The relationships of the retinal fibers to the optic tracts are illustrated below, with the nasal retinal fibers in blue and the temporal retinal fibers in red.
Retinohypothalamic tract	The retinohypothalamic tract is a photic input pathway involved in the circadian rhythms of mammals. The origin of the retinohypothalamic tract is the intrinsically photosensitive retinal ganglion cells (ipRGC), which contain the photopigment melanopsin. The axons of the ipRGCs belonging to the retinohypothalamic tract project directly, monosynaptically, to the suprachiasmatic nuclei via the optic nerve and the optic chiasm.
Melanopsin	Melanopsin is a photopigment found in specialized photosensitive ganglion cells of the retina that are involved in the regulation of circadian rhythms, pupillary light reflex, and other non-visual responses to light. In structure, melanopsin is an opsin, a retinylidene protein variety of G-protein-coupled receptor. Melanopsin is most sensitive to blue light.
Retinal ganglion cell	A retinal ganglion cell is a type of neuron located near the inner surface (the ganglion cell layer) of the retina of the eye. It receives visual information from photoreceptors via two intermediate neuron types: bipolar cells and amacrine cells.

5-Hydroxytryptophan	5-Hydroxytryptophan also known as oxitriptan (INN), is a naturally occurring amino acid and chemical precursor as well as a metabolic intermediate in the biosynthesis of the neurotransmitters serotonin and melatonin from tryptophan. 5-HTP is sold over-the-counter in the United Kingdom, United States and Canada as a dietary supplement for use as an antidepressant, appetite suppressant, and sleep aid, and is also marketed in many European countries for the indication of major depression under trade names like Cincofarm, Levothym, Levotonine, Oxyfan, Telesol, Tript-OH, and Triptum. Several double-blind placebo-controlled clinical trials have demonstrated the effectiveness of 5-HTP in the treatment of depression, though a lack of high quality studies has been noted.
Benzodiazepine	A benzodiazepine is a psychoactive drug whose core chemical structure is the fusion of a benzene ring and a diazepine ring. The first benzodiazepine, chlordiazepoxide (Librium), was discovered accidentally by Leo Sternbach in 1955, and made available in 1960 by Hoffmann-La Roche, which has also marketed diazepam (Valium) since 1963. Benzodiazepines enhance the effect of the neurotransmitter gamma-aminobutyric acid (GABA), which results in sedative, hypnotic (sleep-inducing), anxiolytic (anti-anxiety), anticonvulsant, muscle relaxant and amnesic action.
Hypnotic drugs	Hypnotic drugs are a class of psychoactives whose primary function is to induce sleep and to be used in the treatment of insomnia and in surgical anesthesia. When used in anesthesia to produce and maintain unconsciousness, 'sleep' is metaphorical and there are no regular sleep stages or cyclical natural states; patients rarely recover from anesthesia feeling refreshed and with renewed energy. Because drugs in this class generally produce dose-dependent effects, ranging from anxiolysis to production of unconsciousness, they are often referred to collectively as sedative-hypnotic drugs.
Insomnia	Insomnia is most often defined by an individual's report of sleeping difficulties. While the term is sometimes used in sleep literature to describe a disorder demonstrated by polysomnographic evidence of disturbed sleep, insomnia is often defined as a positive response to either of two questions: 'Do you experience difficulty sleeping?' or 'Do you have difficulty falling or staying asleep?' Thus, insomnia is most often thought of as both a sign and a symptom that can accompany several sleep, medical, and psychiatric disorders, characterized by persistent difficulty falling asleep and/or staying asleep or sleep of poor quality. Insomnia is typically followed by functional impairment while awake.
Pineal gland	The pineal gland is a small endocrine gland in the vertebrate brain.

	It produces the serotonin derivative melatonin, a hormone that affects the modulation of wake/sleep patterns and seasonal functions. Its shape resembles a tiny pine cone (hence its name), and it is located near the center of the brain, between the two hemispheres, tucked in a groove where the two rounded thalamic bodies join.
Raphe nuclei	The raphe nuclei are a moderate-size cluster of nuclei found in the brain stem. Their main function is to release serotonin to the rest of the brain. Selective serotonin reuptake inhibitor (SSRI) antidepressants are believed to act in these nuclei, as well as at their targets.
Stimulant	Stimulants (also referred to as psychostimulants) are psychoactive drugs which induce temporary improvements in either mental or physical function or both. Examples of these kinds of effects may include enhanced alertness, wakefulness, and locomotion, among others. Due to their effects typically having an 'up' quality to them, stimulants are also occasionally referred to as 'uppers'.
Anxiety	Anxiety is a psychological and physiological state characterized by somatic, emotional, cognitive, and behavioral components. The root meaning of the word anxiety is 'to vex or trouble'; in either the absence or presence of psychological stress, anxiety can create feelings of fear, worry, uneasiness and dread. Anxiety is considered to be a normal reaction to stress.
Hypersomnia	Hypersomnia is a disorder characterized by excessive amounts of sleepiness. There are two main categories of hypersomnia: primary hypersomnia and recurrent hypersomnia. Both have the same symptoms but differ in how often they occur.
Melatonin	Melatonin, also known chemically as N-acetyl-5-methoxytryptamine, is a naturally occurring compound found in animals, plants, and microbes. In animals, circulating levels of the hormone melatonin vary in a daily cycle, thereby allowing the entrainment of the circadian rhythms of several biological functions. Many biological effects of melatonin are produced through activation of melatonin receptors, while others are due to its role as a pervasive and powerful antioxidant, with a particular role in the protection of nuclear and mitochondrial DNA. Products containing melatonin have been available over-the-counter in the United States since the mid-1990s.
Anxiolytic	An anxiolytic is a drug used for the treatment of anxiety and its related psychological and physical symptoms. Anxiolytics have been shown to be useful in the treatment of anxiety disorders.

Drug tolerance	Physiological tolerance or drug tolerance is commonly encountered in pharmacology, when a subject's reaction to a specific drug and concentration of the drug is progressively reduced, requiring an increase in concentration to achieve the desired effect. Drug tolerance can involve both psychological drug tolerance and physiological factors. Characteristics of drug tolerance: it is reversible, the rate depends on the particular drug, dosage and frequency of use, differential development occurs for different effects of the same drug.
Narcolepsy	Narcolepsy is a chronic sleep disorder, or dyssomnia, characterized by excessive sleepiness and sleep attacks at inappropriate times, such as while at work. People with narcolepsy often experience disturbed nocturnal sleep and an abnormal daytime sleep pattern, which often is confused with insomnia. Narcoleptics, when falling asleep, generally experience the REM stage of sleep within 5 minutes; whereas most people do not experience REM sleep until an hour or so later.
Sleep apnea	Sleep apnea is a sleep disorder characterized by abnormal pauses in breathing or instances of abnormally low breathing, during sleep. Each pause in breathing, called an apnea, can last from at least ten seconds to minutes, and may occur 5 to 30 times or more an hour. Similarly, each abnormally low breathing event is called a hypopnea.
Castration	Castration is any action, surgical, chemical, or otherwise, by which a male loses the functions of the testicles or a female loses the functions of the ovaries. Humans The practice of castration has its roots before recorded human history. Castration was frequently used for religious or social reasons in certain cultures in Europe, the Middle East, South Asia, Africa, East Asia.
Hallucination	A hallucination, in the broadest sense of the word, is a perception in the absence of a stimulus. In a stricter sense, hallucinations are defined as perceptions in a conscious and awake state in the absence of external stimuli which have qualities of real perception, in that they are vivid, substantial, and located in external objective space. The latter definition distinguishes hallucinations from the related phenomena of dreaming, which does not involve wakefulness; illusion, which involves distorted or misinterpreted real perception; imagery, which does not mimic real perception and is under voluntary control; and pseudohallucination, which does not mimic real perception, but is not under voluntary control.
Orexin	Orexins are the common names given to a pair of excitatory neuropeptide hormones that were simultaneously discovered by two groups of researchers in rat brains.

The two related peptides (Orexin-A and B, or hypocretin-1 and -2), with approximately 50% sequence identity, are produced by cleavage of a single precursor protein. Orexin-A/hypocretin-1 is 33 amino acid residues long and has two intrachain disulfide bonds, while Orexin-B/hypocretin-2 is a linear 28 amino acid residue peptide. Studies suggest that orexin A/hypocretin-1 may be of greater biological importance than orexin B/hypocretin-2. Although these peptides are produced by a very small population of cells in the lateral and posterior hypothalamus, they send projections throughout the brain. The orexin peptides bind to the two G-protein coupled orexin receptors, OX_1 and OX_2, with Orexin-A binding to both OX_1 and OX_2 with approximately equal affinity while Orexin-B binds mainly to OX_2 and is 5 times less potent at OX_1.

Sleep paralysis	Sleep paralysis is paralysis associated with sleep that may occur in healthy persons or may be associated with narcolepsy, cataplexy, and hypnagogic hallucinations. The pathophysiology of this condition is closely related to the normal hypotonia that occurs during REM sleep. When considered to be a disease, isolated sleep paralysis is classified as MeSH D020188. Some evidence suggests that it can also, in some cases, be a symptom of migraine.
Sleep inertia	Sleep inertia is a physiological state characterised by a decline in motor dexterity and a subjective feeling of grogginess immediately following an abrupt awakening. The impaired alertness may interfere with the ability to perform mental or physical tasks. Sleep inertia can also refer to the tendency of a person wanting to return to sleep.
Mortality rate	Mortality rate is a measure of the number of deaths (in general, or due to a specific cause) in some population, scaled to the size of that population, per unit time. Mortality rate is typically expressed in units of deaths per 1000 individuals per year; thus, a mortality rate of 9.5 in a population of 100,000 would mean 950 deaths per year in that entire population, or 0.95% out of the total. It is distinct from morbidity rate, which refers to the number of individuals in poor health during a given time period (the prevalence rate) or the number of newly appearing cases of the disease per unit of time (incidence rate).

1. _____ often referred to as deep sleep, consists of stages 3 and 4 of non-rapid eye movement sleep, according to the Rechtschaffen & Kales (R & K) standard of 1968. As of 2008, the American Academy of Sleep Medicine (AASM) has discontinued the use of stage 4, such that the previous stages 3 and 4 now are combined as stage 3. An epoch (30 seconds of sleep) which consists of 20% or more slow wave (delta) sleep, now is considered to be stage 3.

The highest arousal thresholds (i.e. difficulty of awakening, such as by a sound of a particular volume) are observed in deep sleep. A person will typically feel more groggy when awoken from _____, and indeed, cognitive tests administered after awakening then indicate that mental performance is somewhat impaired for periods of up to 30 minutes or so, relative to awakenings from other stages.

a. Slow-wave sleep
b. Carl Rogers theory evaluation
c. massed learning
d. Sudden infant death syndrome

2. A _____ is a high amplitude brain wave with a frequency of oscillation between 0-4 hertz. _____s, like other brain waves, are recorded with an electroencephalogram (EEG) and are usually associated with the deepest stages of sleep (3 and 4 NREM), also known as slow-wave sleep (SWS), and aid in characterizing the depth of sleep.

a. Carl Rogers theory evaluation
b. Delta wave
c. Posse Comitatus Act
d. Wilkinson v Downton

3. A _____ is a burst of oscillatory brain activity visible on an EEG that occurs during stage 2 sleep. It consists of 12-14 Hz waves that occur for at least 0.5 seconds.

_____s (sometimes referred to as 'sigma bands' or 'sigma waves') may represent periods where the brain is inhibiting processing to keep the sleeper in a tranquil state.

a. Sleepwalking
b. Sleep spindle
c. Sopor
d. Sudden infant death syndrome

4. . _____ is a technique for evaluating and recording the electrical activity produced by skeletal muscles. EMG is performed using an instrument called an electromyograph, to produce a record called an electromyogram. An electromyograph detects the electrical potential generated by muscle cells when these cells are electrically or neurologically activated.

a. Organized Crime Control Act
b. Asia Society
c. Uniform Determination of Death Act

5. _____. is a technique for measuring the resting potential of the retina. The resulting signal is called the electrooculogram.

    a. Electrooculography
    b. Optokinetic drum
    c. Organized Crime Control Act
    d. Asia Society

1. a
2. b
3. b
4. d
5. a

You can take the complete Chapter Practice Test

for Chapter 14. Sleep, Dreaming, and Circadian Rhythms
on all key terms, persons, places, and concepts.

Online 99 Cents

http://www.epub3.10.9241.14.cram101.com/

Use www.Cram101.com for all your study needs

including Cram101's online interactive problem solving labs in

chemistry, statistics, mathematics, and more.

Chapter 15. Drug Addiction and the Brain`s Reward Circuits

CHAPTER OUTLINE: KEY TERMS, PEOPLE, PLACES, CONCEPTS

	Drug addiction
	Injection
	Psychoactive drug
	Drug metabolism
	Drug tolerance
	Antidepressant
	Hypothermia
	Drug overdose
	Amphetamine
	Heroin
	Morphine
	Classical conditioning
	Cannabis sativa
	Cocaine
	Tobacco
	Depressant
	Emphysema
	Apoptosis
	Cannabinoid

Delirium tremens

Dementia

Fetal alcohol syndrome

Hangover

Hash oil

Hashish

Ion channel

Second messenger

Tachycardia

Narcotic

Anandamide

Asthma

Caffeine

Cocaine paste

Lidocaine

Paranoid schizophrenia

Procaine

Schizophrenia

Stimulant

CHAPTER OUTLINE: KEY TERMS, PEOPLE, PLACES, CONCEPTS

Catecholamine

Codeine

Insomnia

MDMA

Opium

Flatulence

Laudanum

Buprenorphine

Endorphin

Methadone

Neuropeptide

Pleasure center

Nigrostriatal pathway

Nucleus accumbens

Parkinson's disease

Substantia nigra

Ventral tegmental area

Dopamine

Dopamine transporter

Chapter 15. Drug Addiction and the Brain`s Reward Circuits

Drug addiction	Substance dependence, commonly called drug addiction, is a drug user's compulsive need to use controlled substances in order to function normally. When such substances are unobtainable, the user suffers from substance withdrawal. The section about substance dependence in the Diagnostic and Statistical Manual of Mental Disorders (more specifically, the 2000 'text revision', the DSM-IV-TR) does not use the word addiction at all.
Injection	An injection (often referred to as a 'shot' or a 'jab') is an infusion method of putting fluid into the body, usually with a hollow needle and a syringe which is pierced through the skin to a sufficient depth for the material to be forced into the body. An injection follows a parenteral route of administration; that is, administered other than through the digestive tract. There are several methods of injection or infusion, including intradermal, subcutaneous, intramuscular, intravenous, intraosseous, and intraperitoneal.
Psychoactive drug	A psychoactive drug, psychopharmaceutical, or psychotropic is a chemical substance that crosses the blood-brain barrier and acts primarily upon the central nervous system where it affects brain function, resulting in changes in perception, mood, consciousness, cognition, and behavior. These substances may be used recreationally, to purposefully alter one's consciousness, as entheogens, for ritual, spiritual, and/or shamanic purposes, as a tool for studying or augmenting the mind, or therapeutically as medication. Because psychoactive substances bring about subjective changes in consciousness and mood that the user may find pleasant (e.g. euphoria) or advantageous (e.g. increased alertness), many psychoactive substances are abused, that is, used excessively, despite the health risks or negative consequences.
Drug metabolism	Drug metabolism is the biochemical modification of pharmaceutical substances by living organisms, usually through specialized enzymatic systems. This is a form of xenobiotic metabolism. Drug metabolism often converts lipophilic chemical compounds into more readily excreted polar products. Its rate is an important determinant of the duration and intensity of the pharmacological action of drugs.
Drug tolerance	Physiological tolerance or drug tolerance is commonly encountered in pharmacology, when a subject's reaction to a specific drug and concentration of the drug is progressively reduced, requiring an increase in concentration to achieve the desired effect. Drug tolerance can involve both psychological drug tolerance and physiological factors. Characteristics of drug tolerance: it is reversible, the rate depends on the particular drug, dosage and frequency of use, differential development occurs for different effects of the same drug.

Antidepressant	Antidepressants, are drugs for the treatment of depression. Despite their name, they are often used to treat other conditions, on- or off-label, for conditions such as anxiety disorders, obsessive compulsive disorder, eating disorders, chronic pain, and some hormone-mediated disorders such as dysmenorrhea, and for snoring, migraines, attention-deficit hyperactivity disorder, (ADHD) substance abuse and occasionally even insomnia. Antidepressants are used either alone or combination with other medications.
Hypothermia	Hypothermia is a condition in which core temperature drops below the required temperature for normal metabolism and body functions which is defined as 35.0 °C (95.0 °F). Body temperature is usually maintained near a constant level of 36.5-37.5 °C (98-100 °F) through biologic homeostasis or thermoregulation. If exposed to cold and the internal mechanisms are unable to replenish the heat that is being lost, a drop in core temperature occurs.
Drug overdose	The term drug overdose describes the ingestion or application of a drug or other substance in quantities greater than are recommended or generally practiced. An overdose may result in a toxic state or death. The word 'overdose' implies that there is a common safe dosage and usage for the drug; therefore, the term is commonly only applied to drugs, not poisons, though even certain poisons are harmless at a low enough dosage.
Amphetamine	Amphetamine or amfetamine (INN) is a psychostimulant drug of the phenethylamine class that produces increased wakefulness and focus in association with decreased fatigue and appetite. Brand names of medications that contain, or metabolize into, amphetamine include Adderall, Dexedrine, Dextrostat, Desoxyn, ProCentra, and Vyvanse, as well as Benzedrine in the past. The drug is also used recreationally and as a performance enhancer.
Heroin	Heroin (diacetylmorphine or morphine diacetate (INN)), also known as diamorphine (BAN), is an opiate analgesic synthesized by C.R Alder Wright in 1874 by adding two acetyl groups to the molecule morphine, a derivative of the opium poppy. When used in medicine it is typically used to treat severe pain, such as that resulting from a heart attack. It is the 3,6-diacetyl ester of morphine, and functions as a morphine prodrug (meaning that it is metabolically converted to morphine inside the body in order for it to work).
Morphine	Morphine (; MS Contin, MSIR, Avinza, Kadian, Oramorph, Roxanol, Kapanol) is a potent opiate analgesic drug that is used to relieve severe pain. It was first isolated in 1804 by Friedrich Sertürner, first distributed by him in 1817, and first commercially sold by Merck in 1827, which at the time was a single small chemists' shop. It was more widely used after the invention of the hypodermic needle in 1857.

Chapter 15. Drug Addiction and the Brain`s Reward Circuits

Classical conditioning	Classical conditioning is a form of learning in which the conditioned stimulus or CS, comes to signal the occurrence of a second stimulus, the unconditioned stimulus or US. (A stimulus is a factor that causes a response in an organism). The US is usually a biologically significant stimulus such as food or pain that elicits a response from the start; this is called the unconditioned response or UR. The CS usually produces no particular response at first, but after conditioning it elicits the conditioned response or CR. Classical conditioning differs from operant or instrumental conditioning, in which behavior emitted by the subject is strengthened or weakened by its consequences (i.e. reward or punishment). Conditioning is usually done by pairing the two stimuli, as in Pavlov's classic experiments.
Cannabis sativa	Cannabis sativa is an annual herbaceous plant in the Cannabaceae family. People have cultivated this herb throughout recorded history as a source of industrial fibre, seed oil, food, recreation, religious and spiritual enlightenment, and medicine. Each part of the plant is harvested differently, depending on the purpose of its use.
Cocaine	Cocaine benzoylmethylecgonine (INN) is a crystalline tropane alkaloid that is obtained from the leaves of the coca plant. The name comes from 'coca' in addition to the alkaloid suffix -ine, forming cocaine. It is a stimulant of the central nervous system, an appetite suppressant, and a topical anesthetic. Specifically, it is a serotonin-norepinephrine-dopamine reuptake inhibitor, which mediates functionality of these neurotransmitters as an exogenous catecholamine transporter ligand. Because of the way it affects the mesolimbic reward pathway, cocaine is addictive.
Tobacco	Tobacco is an agricultural product processed from the leaves of plants in the genus Nicotiana. It can be consumed, used as an organic pesticide and, in the form of nicotine tartrate, used in some medicines. It is most commonly used as a recreational drug, and is a valuable cash crop for countries such as Cuba, China and the United States.
Depressant	Depressants are psychoactive drugs that temporarily reduce the function or activity of a specific part of the body or brain. Examples of these kinds of effects may include anxiolysis, sedation, and hypotension. Due to their effects typically having a 'down' quality to them, depressants are also occasionally referred to as 'downers'.
Emphysema	Emphysema is a long-term, progressive disease of the lungs that primarily causes shortness of breath. In people with emphysema, the tissues necessary to support the physical shape and function of the lungs are destroyed. It is included in a group of diseases called chronic obstructive pulmonary disease or COPD (pulmonary refers to the lungs).
Apoptosis	Apoptosis is the process of programmed cell death (PCD) that may occur in multicellular organisms. Biochemical events lead to characteristic cell changes (morphology) and death.

Cannabinoid	Cannabinoids are a class of diverse chemical compounds that activate cannabinoid receptors. These include the endocannabinoids (produced naturally in the body by humans and animals), the phytocannabinoids (produced by various plants), and synthetic cannabinoids (produced chemically by man). The most notable cannabinoid is the phytocannabinoid Δ^9-tetrahydrocannabinol (THC), the primary psychoactive compound of cannabis.
Delirium tremens	Delirium tremens is an acute episode of delirium that is usually caused by withdrawal from alcohol, first described in 1813. Benzodiazepines are the treatment of choice for delirium tremens. Withdrawal from sedative-hypnotics other than alcohol, such as benzodiazepines, or barbiturates, can also result in seizures, delirium tremens, and death if not properly managed. Withdrawal from other drugs which are not sedative-hypnotics such as caffeine, cocaine, etc.
Dementia	Dementia is a serious loss of global cognitive ability in a previously unimpaired person, beyond what might be expected from normal aging. It may be static, the result of a unique global brain injury, or progressive, resulting in long-term decline due to damage or disease in the body. Although dementia is far more common in the geriatric population, it can occur before the age of 65, in which case it is termed 'early onset dementia'.
Fetal alcohol syndrome	Fetal alcohol syndrome is a pattern of mental and physical defects that can develop in a fetus in association with high levels of alcohol consumption during pregnancy. Current research also implicates other lifestyle choices made by the prospective mother. Indications for lower levels of alcohol are inconclusive.
Hangover	A hangover describes the sum of unpleasant physiological effects following heavy consumption of alcoholic beverages. The most commonly reported characteristics of a hangover include headache, nausea, sensitivity to light and noise, lethargy, dysphoria, diarrhea and thirst, typically after the intoxicating effects of the alcohol begin to wear off. While a hangover can be experienced at any time, generally speaking a hangover is experienced the morning after a night of heavy drinking.
Hash oil	Hash oil is a resinous matrix of cannabinoids produced by a solvent extraction of cannabis. Hash oil is a concentrated product with a high THC content, which generally varies between 40% and 90%. Related honey oil is a specific type of hash oil made from the more potent parts of the cannabis plant.
Hashish	Hashish, often known as 'hash', is a cannabis preparation composed of compressed and/or purified preparations of stalked resin glands, called trichomes, collected from the unfertilized buds of the cannabis plant. It contains the same active ingredients - such as THC and other cannabinoids - but in higher concentrations than unsifted buds or leaves.

Chapter 15. Drug Addiction and the Brain`s Reward Circuits

Ion channel	Ion channels are pore-forming proteins that help establish and control the voltage gradient across the plasma membrane of cells by allowing the flow of ions down their electrochemical gradient. They are present in the membranes that surround all biological cells. The study of ion channels involves many scientific techniques such as voltage clamp electrophysiology (in particular patch clamp), immunohistochemistry, and RT-PCR. Ion channels regulate the flow of ions across the membrane in all cells.
Second messenger	Second messengers are molecules that relay signals from receptors on the cell surface to target molecules inside the cell, in the cytoplasm or nucleus. They relay the signals of hormones like epinephrine (adrenaline), growth factors, and others, and cause some kind of change in the activity of the cell. They greatly amplify the strength of the signal.
Tachycardia	Tachycardia comes from the Greek words tachys (rapid or accelerated) and kardia (of the heart). Tachycardia typically refers to a heart rate that exceeds the normal range for a resting heartrate (heartrate in an inactive or sleeping individual). It can be dangerous depending on the speed and type of rhythm.
Narcotic	The term narcotic originally referred medically to any psychoactive compound with sleep-inducing properties. In the United States of America it has since become associated with opioids, commonly morphine and heroin. The term is, today, imprecisely defined and typically has negative connotations.
Anandamide	Anandamide, is an endogenous cannabinoid neurotransmitter. The name is taken from the Sanskrit word ananda, which means 'bliss, delight', and amide. It is synthesized from N-arachidonoyl phosphatidylethanolamine by multiple pathways.
Asthma	Asthma is a common chronic inflammatory disease of the airways characterized by variable and recurring symptoms, reversible airflow obstruction, and bronchospasm. Common symptoms include wheezing, coughing, chest tightness, and shortness of breath. Asthma is thought to be caused by a combination of genetic and environmental factors.
Caffeine	Caffeine is a bitter, white crystalline xanthine alkaloid that acts as a stimulant drug. Caffeine is found in varying quantities in the seeds, leaves, and fruit of some plants, where it acts as a natural pesticide that paralyzes and kills certain insects feeding on the plants. It is most commonly consumed by humans in infusions extracted from the seed of the coffee plant and the leaves of the tea bush, as well as from various foods and drinks containing products derived from the kola nut.

Cocaine paste	Cocaine paste, paco or basuco in South America, short for pasta de cocaína (cocaine paste) or pasta base de cocaína (PBC, cocaine base paste), is a collective name given to several different cocaine products. Cocaine paste includes crude intermediate stages of the cocaine preparation process and their freebase forms as well as 'crack cocaine' prepared from pure cocaine hydrochloride. Crude cocaine preparation intermediates are marketed as cheaper alternatives to pure cocaine to local markets while the more expensive end product is exported to US and European markets.
Lidocaine	Lidocaine is a common local anesthetic and antiarrhythmic drug. Lidocaine is used topically to relieve itching, burning and pain from skin inflammations, injected as a dental anesthetic or as a local anesthetic for minor surgery. Lidocaine, the first amino amide-type local anesthetic, was first synthesized under the name Xylocaine by Swedish chemist Nils Löfgren in 1943. His colleague Bengt Lundqvist performed the first injection anesthesia experiments on himself.
Paranoid schizophrenia	Paranoid schizophrenia is a sub-type of schizophrenia. In the United States, it is defined in the Diagnostic and Statistical Manual of Mental Disorders, DSM-IV code 295.30. It is the most common type of schizophrenia. Aspects Paranoid schizophrenia is manifested primarily through impaired thought processes, in which the central focus is on distorted perceptions or paranoid behavior and thinking.
Procaine	Procaine is a local anesthetic drug of the amino ester group. It is used primarily to reduce the pain of intramuscular injection of penicillin, and it was also used in dentistry. Owing to the ubiquity of the trade name Novocain, in some regions procaine is referred to generically as novocaine. It acts mainly by being a sodium channel blocker.
Schizophrenia	Schizophrenia is a mental disorder characterized by a disintegration of thought processes and of emotional responsiveness. It most commonly manifests as auditory hallucinations, paranoid or bizarre delusions, or disorganized speech and thinking, and it is accompanied by significant social or occupational dysfunction. The onset of symptoms typically occurs in young adulthood, with a global lifetime prevalence of about 0.3-0.7%.
Stimulant	Stimulants (also referred to as psychostimulants) are psychoactive drugs which induce temporary improvements in either mental or physical function or both. Examples of these kinds of effects may include enhanced alertness, wakefulness, and locomotion, among others.

Catecholamine	Catecholamines are 'fight-or-flight' hormones released by the adrenal glands in response to stress. They are part of the sympathetic nervous system. They are called catecholamines because they contain a catechol or 3,4-dihydroxylphenyl group.
Codeine	Codeine, the other being the semi-synthetic 6-methylmorphine) is an opiate used for its analgesic, antitussive, and antidiarrheal properties. Codeine is the second-most predominant alkaloid in opium, at up to three percent; it is much more prevalent in the Iranian poppy (Papaver bractreatum), and codeine is extracted from this species in some places although the below-mentioned morphine methylation process is still much more common. It is considered the prototype of the weak to midrange opioids (tramadol, dextropropoxyphene, dihydrocodeine, hydrocodone).
Insomnia	Insomnia is most often defined by an individual's report of sleeping difficulties. While the term is sometimes used in sleep literature to describe a disorder demonstrated by polysomnographic evidence of disturbed sleep, insomnia is often defined as a positive response to either of two questions: 'Do you experience difficulty sleeping?' or 'Do you have difficulty falling or staying asleep?' Thus, insomnia is most often thought of as both a sign and a symptom that can accompany several sleep, medical, and psychiatric disorders, characterized by persistent difficulty falling asleep and/or staying asleep or sleep of poor quality. Insomnia is typically followed by functional impairment while awake.
MDMA	MDMA - colloquially known as ecstasy, often abbreviated 'E' or 'X' - is an entactogenic drug of the phenethylamine and amphetamine class of drugs. MDMA can induce euphoria, a sense of intimacy with others, and diminished anxiety and depression. Many, particularly in the fields of psychology and cognitive therapy, have suggested MDMA might have therapeutic benefits and facilitate therapy sessions in certain individuals, a practice which it had formally been used for in the past.
Opium	Opium is the dried latex obtained from the opium poppy (Papaver somniferum). Opium contains up to 12% morphine, an alkaloid, which is frequently processed chemically to produce heroin for the illegal drug trade. The latex also includes codeine and non-narcotic alkaloids such as papaverine, thebaine and noscapine.
Flatulence	Flatulence is the expulsion through the rectum of a mixture of gases that are byproducts of the digestion process of mammals and other animals. The medical term for the mixture of gases is flatus, informally known as a fart, or simply gas. The gases are expelled from the rectum in a process colloquially referred to as 'passing gas', 'breaking wind' or 'farting'.

Laudanum	Laudanum is an alcoholic herbal preparation containing approximately 10% powdered opium by weight (the equivalent of 1% morphine). It is reddish-brown in color and extremely bitter to the taste. Laudanum contains almost all of the opium alkaloids, including morphine and codeine. A potent narcotic by virtue of its high morphine concentration, laudanum was historically used to treat a variety of ailments, but its principal use was as an analgesic and cough suppressant.
Buprenorphine	Buprenorphine is a semi-synthetic opioid that is used to treat opioid addiction in higher dosages (>2 mg), to control moderate acute pain in non-opioid-tolerant individuals in lower dosages (~200 µg), and to control moderate chronic pain in dosages ranging from 20-70 µg/hour. It is available in a variety of formulations: Subutex, Suboxone (typically used for opioid addiction), Temgesic, Buprenex (solutions for injection often used for acute pain in primary-care settings), Norspan and Butrans (transdermal preparations used for chronic pain).
	Buprenorphine hydrochloride was first marketed in the 1980s by Reckitt & Colman (now Reckitt Benckiser) as an analgesic, generally available as Temgesic 0.2 mg sublingual tablets, and as Buprenex in a 0.3 mg/ml injectable formulation.
Endorphin	Endorphins ('endogenous morphine') are endogenous opioid peptides that function as neurotransmitters. They are produced by the pituitary gland and the hypothalamus in vertebrates during exercise, excitement, pain, consumption of spicy food, love and orgasm, and they resemble the opiates in their abilities to produce analgesia and a feeling of well-being.
	The term implies a pharmacological activity (analogous to the activity of the corticosteroid category of biochemicals) as opposed to a specific chemical formulation.
Methadone	Methadone is a synthetic opioid, used medically as an analgesic and a maintenance anti-addictive for use in patients with opioid dependency. It was developed in Germany in 1937. Although chemically unlike morphine or heroin, methadone acts on the same opioid receptors as these drugs, and thus has many of the same effects. Methadone is also used in managing severe chronic pain, owing to its long duration of action, extremely powerful effects, and very low cost.
Neuropeptide	Neuropeptides are small protein-like molecules used by neurons to communicate with each other, distinct from the larger neurotransmitters. They are neuronal signaling molecules, influence the activity of the brain in specific ways and are thus involved in particular brain functions, like analgesia, reward, food intake, learning and memory.
	Neuropeptides are expressed and released by neurons, and mediate or modulate neuronal communication by acting on cell surface receptors.
Pleasure center	Pleasure center is the general term used for the brain regions involved in pleasure.

Chapter 15. Drug Addiction and the Brain's Reward Circuits

	Discoveries made in the 1950s initially suggested that rodents could not stop electrically stimulating parts of their brain, mainly the nucleus accumbens, which was theorized to produce great pleasure. Further investigations revealed that the septum pellucidium and the hypothalamus can also be targets for self-stimulation.
Nigrostriatal pathway	Dopaminergic pathways are neural pathways in the brain which transmit the neurotransmitter dopamine from one region of the brain to another. The nigrostriatal pathway is a neural pathway that connects the substantia nigra with the striatum. It is one of the four major dopamine pathways in the brain, and is particularly involved in the production of movement, as part of a system called the basal ganglia motor loop.
Nucleus accumbens	The nucleus accumbens also known as the accumbens nucleus or as the nucleus accumbens septi, is a collection of neurons and forms the main part of the ventral striatum. It is thought to play an important role in reward, pleasure, laughter, addiction, aggression, fear, and the placebo effect. Each half of the brain has one nucleus accumbens.
Parkinson's disease	Parkinson's disease is a degenerative disorder of the central nervous system. It results from the death of dopamine-containing cells in the substantia nigra, a region of the midbrain; the cause of cell-death is unknown. Early in the course of the disease, the most obvious symptoms are movement-related, including shaking, rigidity, slowness of movement and difficulty with walking and gait. Later, cognitive and behavioural problems may arise, with dementia commonly occurring in the advanced stages of the disease. Other symptoms include sensory, sleep and emotional problems. Parkinson's disease is more common in the elderly with most cases occurring after the age of 50.
Substantia nigra	The substantia nigra is a brain structure located in the mesencephalon (midbrain) that plays an important role in reward, addiction, and movement. Substantia nigra is Latin for 'black substance', as parts of the substantia nigra appear darker than neighboring areas due to high levels of melanin in dopaminergic neurons. Parkinson's disease is caused by the death of dopaminergic neurons in the substantia nigra pars compacta.
Ventral tegmental area	The ventral tegmentum, better known as the ventral tegmental area is a group of neurons located close to the midline on the floor of the midbrain (mesencephalon). The ventral tegmental area is the origin of the dopaminergic cell bodies of the mesocorticolimbic dopamine system and is widely implicated in the drug and natural reward circuitry of the brain. It is important in cognition, motivation, drug addiction, intense emotions relating to love, and several psychiatric disorders.

Chapter 15. Drug Addiction and the Brain`s Reward Circuits

Dopamine	Dopamine, a simple organic chemical in the catecholamine family, plays a number of important physiological roles in the bodies of animals. Its name derives from its chemical structure, which consists of an amine group (NH_2) linked to a catechol structure called dihydroxyphenethylamine, the decarboxyalted form of dihydroxyphenylalanine (acronym DOPA). In the brain, dopamine functions as a neurotransmitter--a chemical released by nerve cells to send signals to other nerve cells.
Dopamine transporter	The dopamine transporter is a membrane-spanning protein that pumps the neurotransmitter dopamine out of the synapse back into cytosol, from which other transporters sequester DA and NE into vesicles for later storage and release. Dopamine reuptake via DAT provides the primary mechanism through which dopamine is cleared from synapses, although there may be an exception in the prefrontal cortex, where evidence points to a possibly larger role of the norepinephrine transporter. DAT is thought to be implicated in a number of dopamine-related disorders, including attention deficit hyperactivity disorder, bipolar disorder, clinical depression, and alcoholism.

1. _____s are a class of diverse chemical compounds that activate _____ receptors. These include the endo_____s (produced naturally in the body by humans and animals), the phyto_____s (produced by various plants), and synthetic _____s (produced chemically by man). The most notable _____ is the phyto_____ Δ^9-tetrahydrocannabinol (THC), the primary psychoactive compound of cannabis.

   a. Signaling Gateway
   b. Asystole
   c. Ataxic respiration
   d. Cannabinoid

2. _____ is the general term used for the brain regions involved in pleasure. Discoveries made in the 1950s initially suggested that rodents could not stop electrically stimulating parts of their brain, mainly the nucleus accumbens, which was theorized to produce great pleasure. Further investigations revealed that the septum pellucidium and the hypothalamus can also be targets for self-stimulation.

   a. Carl Rogers theory evaluation
   b. Big dynorphin
   c. Bombesin
   d. Pleasure center

3. . _____ is a common local anesthetic and antiarrhythmic drug.

Chapter 15. Drug Addiction and the Brain's Reward Circuits

_____ is used topically to relieve itching, burning and pain from skin inflammations, injected as a dental anesthetic or as a local anesthetic for minor surgery.

_____, the first amino amide-type local anesthetic, was first synthesized under the name Xylocaine by Swedish chemist Nils Löfgren in 1943. His colleague Bengt Lundqvist performed the first injection anesthesia experiments on himself.

a. Zanamivir
b. Carl Rogers theory evaluation
c. Lidocaine
d. Crack stem

4. _____ is a long-term, progressive disease of the lungs that primarily causes shortness of breath. In people with _____, the tissues necessary to support the physical shape and function of the lungs are destroyed. It is included in a group of diseases called chronic obstructive pulmonary disease or COPD (pulmonary refers to the lungs).

a. Inflight smoking
b. Action on Smoking and Health
c. Ashtray
d. Emphysema

5. _____ or amfetamine (INN) is a psychostimulant drug of the phenethylamine class that produces increased wakefulness and focus in association with decreased fatigue and appetite.

Brand names of medications that contain, or metabolize into, _____ include Adderall, Dexedrine, Dextrostat, Desoxyn, ProCentra, and Vyvanse, as well as Benzedrine in the past.

The drug is also used recreationally and as a performance enhancer.

a. AR-R17779
b. Armodafinil
c. Amphetamine
d. ECA stack

1. d

2. d

3. c

4. d

5. c

You can take the complete Chapter Practice Test

for Chapter 15. Drug Addiction and the Brain`s Reward Circuits
on all key terms, persons, places, and concepts.

Online 99 Cents

http://www.epub3.10.9241.15.cram101.com/

Use www.Cram101.com for all your study needs

including Cram101's online interactive problem solving labs in

chemistry, statistics, mathematics, and more.

Chapter 16. Lateralization, Language, and the Split Brain

CHAPTER OUTLINE: KEY TERMS, PEOPLE, PLACES, CONCEPTS

Cerebral hemisphere

Corpus callosum

Aphasia

Apraxia

Broca's area

Dichotic listening test

Muteness

Wechsler Adult Intelligence Scale

Scotoma

Split-brain

Convulsion

Chimera

Spatial cognition

Brain function lateralization

Planum temporale

Wernicke's area

Cerebrum

American sign language

Deafness

Chapter 16. Lateralization, Language, and the Split Brain

Agraphia

Angular gyrus

Arcuate fasciculus

Broca's aphasia

Conduction aphasia

Wernicke-Geschwind model

Word salad

Primary auditory cortex

Cerebral edema

Edema

X-ray computed tomography

Global aphasia

Adrenal cortex

Epilepsy

Cognition

Semantic analysis

Dyslexia

Deep dyslexia

Surface dyslexia

| | Hemispherectomy |

Cerebral hemisphere	A cerebral hemisphere is one of the two regions of the eutherian brain that are delineated by the median plane, (medial longitudinal fissure). The brain can thus be described as being divided into left and right cerebral hemispheres. Each of these hemispheres has an outer layer of grey matter called the cerebral cortex that is supported by an inner layer of white matter.
Corpus callosum	The corpus callosum, is a wide, flat bundle of neural fibers beneath the cortex in the eutherian brain at the longitudinal fissure. It connects the left and right cerebral hemispheres and facilitates interhemispheric communication. It is the largest white matter structure in the brain, consisting of 200-250 million contralateral axonal projections.
Aphasia	Aphasia meaning speechless, is an acquired language disorder in which there is an impairment of any language modality. This may include difficulty in producing or comprehending spoken or written language. In technical terms, aphasia suggests the total impairment of language ability, and dysphasia a degree of impairment less than total.
Apraxia	Apraxia is characterized by loss of the ability to execute or carry out learned purposeful movements, despite having the desire and the physical ability to perform the movements. It is a disorder of motor planning, which may be acquired or developmental, but is not caused by incoordination, sensory loss, or failure to comprehend simple commands (which can be tested by asking the person to recognize the correct movement from a series). It is caused by damage to specific areas of the cerebrum.
Broca's area	Broca's area is a region of the hominid brain with functions linked to speech production.
Dichotic listening test	In cognitive psychology and neuroscience, dichotic listening is a procedure commonly used to investigate selective attention in the auditory system. More specifically, it is 'used as a behavioral test for hemispheric lateralization of speech sound perception.' During a standard dichotic listening test, a participant is simultaneously presented with two different auditory stimuli (usually speech) separately to each ear over headphones.

Chapter 16. Lateralization, Language, and the Split Brain

Muteness	Muteness is a kind of speech disorder that causes an inability to speak. The term mute originates from the latin word mutus, for silent. Causes and variations Selective mutism is a DSM-IV diagnosis that refers to an anxiety disorder in which people are unable to speak in situations causing social anxiety, but are fluent in speech in more comfortable situations.
Wechsler Adult Intelligence Scale	The Wechsler Adult Intelligence Scale is a test designed to measure intelligence in adults and older adolescents. It is currently in its fourth edition (WAIS-IV). The original WAIS (Form I) was published in February 1955 by David Wechsler, as a revision of the Wechsler-Bellevue Intelligence Scale.
Scotoma	A scotoma is an area of partial alteration in one's field of vision consisting of a partially diminished or entirely degenerated visual acuity which is surrounded by a field of normal - or relatively well-preserved - vision. Every normal mammalian eye has a scotoma in its field of vision, usually termed its blind spot. This is a location with no photoreceptor cells, where the retinal ganglion cell axons that comprise the optic nerve exit the retina.
Split-brain	Split-brain is a lay term to describe the result when the corpus callosum connecting the two hemispheres of the brain is severed to some degree. It is an association of symptoms produced by disruption of or interference with the connection between the hemispheres of the brain. The surgical operation to produce this condition is called corpus callosotomy (not to be confused with colostomy) and is usually used as a last resort to treat otherwise intractable epilepsy.
Convulsion	A convulsion is a medical condition where body muscles contract and relax rapidly and repeatedly, resulting in an uncontrolled shaking of the body. Because a convulsion is often a symptom of an epileptic seizure, the term convulsion is sometimes used as a synonym for seizure. However, not all epileptic seizures lead to convulsions, and not all convulsions are caused by epileptic seizures.
Chimera	A chimera or chimaera is a single organism (usually an animal) that is composed of two or more different populations of genetically distinct cells that originated from different zygotes involved in sexual reproduction. If the different cells have emerged from the same zygote, the organism is called a mosaic. Chimeras are formed from at least four parent cells (two fertilized eggs or early embryos fused together).

Spatial cognition	Spatial cognition is concerned with the acquisition, organization, utilization, and revision of knowledge about spatial environments. These capabilities enable humans to manage basic and high-level cognitive tasks in everyday life. Numerous disciplines (such as Psychology, Geographic Information Science, Artificial Intelligence, Cartography, etc).
Brain function lateralization	Brain function lateralization is evident in the phenomena of right- or left-handedness and of right or left ear preference, but a person's preferred hand is not a clear indication of the location of brain function. Although 95% of right-handed people have left-hemisphere dominance for language, 18.8% of left-handed people have right-hemisphere dominance for language function. Additionally, 19.8% of the left-handed have bilateral language functions. Even within various language functions (e.g., semantics, syntax, prosody), degree (and even hemisphere) of dominance may differ.
Planum temporale	The planum temporale is an area of the human brain. It is the cortical area just posterior to the auditory cortex (Heschl's gyrus) within the Sylvian fissure. It is a triangular region which forms the heart of Wernicke's area, one of the most important functional areas for language.
Wernicke's area	Wernicke's area is one of the two parts of the cerebral cortex linked since the late nineteenth century to speech (the other is Broca's area). It is involved in the understanding of written and spoken language. It is traditionally considered to consist of the posterior section of the superior temporal gyrus in the dominant cerebral hemisphere (which is the left hemisphere in about 90% of people).
Cerebrum	The cerebrum, together with the diencephalon, constitutes the forebrain. In humans, the cerebrum is the most superior region of the vertebrate central nervous system. However, in the majority of animals, the cerebrum is the most anterior region of the CNS as the anatomical position of animals is rarely in the upright position.
American sign language	American Sign Language is the dominant sign language of Deaf Americans . It is the third most used language in the United States next to English and Spanish. Although the United Kingdom and the United States share English as a spoken and written language, British Sign Language (BSL) is quite different from American Sign Language, and the two sign languages are not mutually intelligible. American Sign Language, however, derived from French Sign Language.
Deafness	Deafness, is a partial or total inability to hear where the ability would usually be expected. Hearing sensitivity is indicated by the quietest sound that an animal can detect, called the hearing threshold. In the case of humans and some animals, this threshold can be accurately measured by a behavioral audiogram.
Agraphia	Agraphia is inability to write resulting from brain disease.

	Agraphia is a type of aphasia, which is an absent or impaired language ability. Causes
	It results from a damage to the Wernicke's Area of the brain, which includes the brodmann's areas 39 and 40 of parietal lobe, and area 22 of temporal lobe.
Angular gyrus	The angular gyrus is a region of the brain in the parietal lobe, that lies near the superior edge of the temporal lobe, and immediately posterior to the supramarginal gyrus; it is involved in a number of processes related to language, mathematics and cognition. It is Brodmann area 39 of the human brain. Language
	Geschwind proposed that written word is translated to internal monologue via the angular gyrus.
Arcuate fasciculus	The arcuate fasciculus is the neural pathway connecting the posterior part of the temporoparietal junction with the frontal cortex in the brain and is now considered as part of the superior longitudinal fasciculus.. Neuroanatomy
	While previously thought to connect Wernicke's area and Broca's area, new research demonstrates that the arcuate fasciculus instead connects posterior receptive areas with premotor/motor areas, and not to Broca's area.
	Although the regions the arcuate fasciculus connects to is a topic still in debate, the 'connectivity' of the arcuate has been shown to correspond to various functional areas within the temporal, parietal, and frontal lobes As fractional anisotropy of the arcuate increases, cortical thickness increases in corresponding areas.
Broca's aphasia	Broca's aphasia in clinical neuropsychology and agrammatic aphasia in cognitive neuropsychology, is caused by damage to or developmental issues in anterior regions of the brain, including (but not limited to) the left posterior inferior frontal gyrus known as Broca's area (Brodmann area 44 and Brodmann area 45). Expressive aphasia is one subset of a larger family of disorders known collectively as aphasia. It is characterized by the loss of the ability to produce language (spoken or written).
Conduction aphasia	Conduction aphasia, is a relatively rare form of aphasia. An acquired language disorder, it is characterized by intact auditory comprehension, fluent (yet paraphasic) speech production, but poor speech repetition. They are fully capable of understanding what they are hearing but they will have difficulty repeating what was actually said.
Wernicke-Geschwind model	Carl Wernicke created an early neurological model of language, that later was revived by Norman Geschwind. The model is known as the Wernicke-Geschwind model. •For listening to and understanding spoken words, the sounds of the words are sent through the auditory pathways to area 41, which is the primary auditory cortex (Heschl's gyrus).

From there, they continue to Wernicke's area, where the meaning of the words is extracted.•In order to speak, the meanings of words are sent from Wernicke's area via the arcuate fasciculus to Broca's area, where morphemes are assembled. The model proposes that Broca's area holds a representation for articulating words. Instructions for speech are sent from Broca's area to the facial area of the motor cortex, and from there instructions are sent to facial motor neurons in the brainstem, which relay movement orders to facial muscles.•In order to read, information concerning the written text is sent from visual areas 17, 18, and 19 to the angular gyrus (area 39) and from there to Wernicke's area, for silent reading or, together with Broca's area, for reading out loud.

This model is now obsolete. Nevertheless it has been very useful in directing research and organizing research results, because it is based on the idea that language consists of two basic functions: comprehension, which is a sensory/perceptual function, and speaking, which is a motor function.However, the neural organization of language is more complex than the Wernicke-Geschwind model of language suggests. The localization of speech in Broca's area is one of the weakest points of this model.

Word salad	Word salad is a mixture of random words that, while arranged in phrases that appear to give them meaning, actually carry no significance. The words may or may not be grammatically correct, but the meaning is hopelessly confused. A famous example is Noam Chomsky's phrase, 'Colorless green ideas sleep furiously.' The term is used to describe poetry and other literary works (as in Chomsky's example), but is also often used to describe a symptom of mental disorders or textual randomization in computer programs.
Primary auditory cortex	The primary auditory cortex is a region of the brain that processes sound and thereby contributes to our ability to hear. It is the first cortical region of the auditory pathway. Corresponding roughly with Brodmann areas 41 and 42 of the cerebral cortex, it is located on the temporal lobe, and performs the basics of hearing--pitch and volume.
Cerebral edema	Cerebral edema is an excess accumulation of water in the intracellular or extracellular spaces of the brain. Four types of cerebral edema have been distinguished:Vasogenic Due to a breakdown of tight endothelial junctions which make up the blood-brain barrier (BBB). This allows normally excluded intravascular proteins and fluid to penetrate into cerebral parenchymal extracellular space.
Edema	Edema, formerly known as dropsy or hydropsy, is an abnormal accumulation of fluid beneath the skin or in one or more cavities of the body.

Generally, the amount of interstitial fluid is determined by the balance of fluid homeostasis, and increased secretion of fluid into the interstitium or impaired removal of this fluid may cause edema.

Classification

Cutaneous edema is referred to as 'pitting' when after pressure is applied to a small area, the indentation persists for some time after the release of the pressure.

| X-ray computed tomography | X-ray computed tomography is a medical imaging method employing tomography created by computer processing. Digital geometry processing is used to generate a three-dimensional image of the inside of an object from a large series of two-dimensional X-ray images taken around a single axis of rotation.

X-ray computed tomography produces a volume of data which can be manipulated, through a process known as 'windowing', in order to demonstrate various bodily structures based on their ability to block the X-ray beam. |
|---|---|
| Global aphasia | Global aphasia is a type of aphasia that is commonly associated with a large lesion in the perisylvian area of the frontal, temporal and parietal lobes of the brain causing an almost total reduction of all aspects of spoken and written language. It involves a 'left side blowout' which includes Broca's area, Wernicke's area and the Arcuate fasciculus. It can also be seen in the initial stages of large left middle cerebral artery injuries that may progressively improve to become expressive aphasia. |
| Adrenal cortex | Situated along the perimeter of the adrenal gland, the adrenal cortex mediates the stress response through the production of mineralocorticoids and glucocorticoids, including aldosterone and cortisol respectively. It is also a secondary site of androgen synthesis. |
| Epilepsy | Epilepsy is a common and diverse set of chronic neurological disorders characterized by seizures. Some definitions of epilepsy require that seizures be recurrent and unprovoked, but others require only a single seizure combined with brain alterations which increase the chance of future seizures. In many cases a cause cannot be identified; however, factors that are associated include brain trauma, strokes, brain cancer, and drug and alcohol misuse among others. |
| Cognition | In science, cognition is a group of mental processes that includes attention, memory, producing and understanding language, solving problems, and making decisions. Cognition is studied in various disciplines such as psychology, philosophy, linguistics, science and computer science. |

Semantic analysis	In linguistics, semantic analysis is the process of relating syntactic structures, from the levels of phrases, clauses, sentences and paragraphs to the level of the writing as a whole, to their language-independent meanings. It also involves removing features specific to particular linguistic and cultural contexts, to the extent that such a project is possible. The elements of idiom and figurative speech, being cultural, are often also converted into relatively invariant meanings in semantic analysis.
Dyslexia	Dyslexia is a very broad term defining a learning disability that impairs a person's fluency or comprehension accuracy in being able to read, and which can manifest itself as a difficulty with phonological awareness, phonological decoding, orthographic coding, auditory short-term memory, or rapid naming.
	Dyslexia is distinct from reading difficulties resulting from other causes, such as a non-neurological deficiency with vision or hearing, or from poor or inadequate reading instruction. It is believed that dyslexia can affect between 5 and 10 percent of a given population although there have been no studies to indicate an accurate percentage.
Deep dyslexia	Deep dyslexia is a form of alexia that disrupts reading processes that were functioning normally before the individual suffered a head trauma to the dominant hemisphere (usually left). Deep dyslexia may occur as a result of a head injury, stroke, disease, or operation.
	The term dyslexia comes from the Greek words 'dys' meaning 'impaired', and 'lexis' meaning 'word' and is used to describe disorders of language concerning reading and spelling.
Surface dyslexia	Surface dyslexia is one type of Alexia (acquired dyslexia) that patients have a reading disorder.
	According to Marshall & Newcombe's (1973) and McCarthy & Warrington's study (1990), this kind of disorder is that patients cannot recognize the word as a whole due to the damage of the left parietal or temporal lobe. This means they will make mistakes once the visual appearance--the spelling--of the word is not in accordance with the pronunciation rules.
Hemispherectomy	Hemispherectomy is a very rare surgical procedure where one cerebral hemisphere (half of the brain) is removed or disabled. This procedure is used to treat a variety of seizure disorders where the source of the epilepsy is localized to a broad area of a single hemisphere of the brain, among other disorders. It is solely reserved for extreme cases in which the seizures have not responded to medications and other less invasive surgeries.

Chapter 16. Lateralization, Language, and the Split Brain

1. _____ is the dominant sign language of Deaf Americans . It is the third most used language in the United States next to English and Spanish. Although the United Kingdom and the United States share English as a spoken and written language, British Sign Language (BSL) is quite different from _____, and the two sign languages are not mutually intelligible. _____, however, derived from French Sign Language.

   a. Organized Crime Control Act
   b. Betz cell
   c. Body of lateral ventricle
   d. American sign language

2. _____ is evident in the phenomena of right- or left-handedness and of right or left ear preference, but a person's preferred hand is not a clear indication of the location of brain function. Although 95% of right-handed people have left-hemisphere dominance for language, 18.8% of left-handed people have right-hemisphere dominance for language function. Additionally, 19.8% of the left-handed have bilateral language functions. Even within various language functions (e.g., semantics, syntax, prosody), degree (and even hemisphere) of dominance may differ.

   a. Carl Rogers theory evaluation
   b. Brain function lateralization
   c. State
   d. Stream of consciousness

3. In science, _____ is a group of mental processes that includes attention, memory, producing and understanding language, solving problems, and making decisions. _____ is studied in various disciplines such as psychology, philosophy, linguistics, science and computer science. The term's usage varies in different disciplines; for example in psychology and cognitive science, it usually refers to an information processing view of an individual's psychological functions.

   a. Cognition
   b. Cognitive anthropology
   c. Cognitive approaches to grammar
   d. Cognitive ethology

4. The _____ is a region of the brain that processes sound and thereby contributes to our ability to hear. It is the first cortical region of the auditory pathway. Corresponding roughly with Brodmann areas 41 and 42 of the cerebral cortex, it is located on the temporal lobe, and performs the basics of hearing--pitch and volume.

   a. Reflex bradycardia
   b. Rosenthal fiber
   c. Samantha Dickson Brain Tumour Trust
   d. Primary auditory cortex

5. . _____ is characterized by loss of the ability to execute or carry out learned purposeful movements, despite having the desire and the physical ability to perform the movements.

It is a disorder of motor planning, which may be acquired or developmental, but is not caused by incoordination, sensory loss, or failure to comprehend simple commands (which can be tested by asking the person to recognize the correct movement from a series). It is caused by damage to specific areas of the cerebrum.

a. Organized Crime Control Act

b. Cortical map

c. Cortical minicolumn

d. Apraxia

1. d
2. b
3. a
4. d
5. d

You can take the complete Chapter Practice Test

for Chapter 16. Lateralization, Language, and the Split Brain
on all key terms, persons, places, and concepts.

Online 99 Cents

http://www.epub3.10.9241.16.cram101.com/

Use www.Cram101.com for all your study needs

including Cram101's online interactive problem solving labs in

chemistry, statistics, mathematics, and more.

	Somatic nervous system
	Amygdala
	Limbic system
	Olfactory bulb
	Lie detection
	Facial expression
	Facial feedback hypothesis
	Electromyography
	Facial electromyography
	Microexpression
	Castration
	Chronic stress
	Convergence
	Stressor
	Adrenal cortex
	Adrenal medulla
	Adrenocorticotropic hormone
	Dominance hierarchy
	Epinephrine

Glucocorticoid

Adrenal glands

Antibody

Cell-mediated immunity

Macrophage

Psychoneuroimmunology

Meta-analysis

Neuropeptide

Spandrel

Granule cell

Prenatal stress

Neurogenesis

Estradiol

Fear conditioning

Periaqueductal gray

Prosody

Extraversion-introversion

Neuroticism

Somatic nervous system	The somatic nervous system is the part of the peripheral nervous system associated with the voluntary control of body movements via skeletal muscles. The SoNS consists of efferent nerves responsible for stimulating muscle contraction, including all the non-sensory neurons connected with skeletal muscles and skin. Parts of Somatic Nervous System
	There are 43 segments of nerves in our body and with each segment there is a pair of sensory and motor nerves.
Amygdala	The are almond-shaped groups of nuclei located deep within the medial temporal lobes of the brain in complex vertebrates, including humans. Shown in research to perform a primary role in the processing of memory and emotional reactions, the amygdalae are considered part of the limbic system. Anatomical subdivisions
	The regions described as amygdala nuclei encompass several structures with distinct connectional and functional characteristics in animals and humans.
Limbic system	The limbic system is a set of brain structures, including the hippocampus, amygdalae, anterior thalamic nuclei, septum, limbic cortex and fornix, which seemingly support a variety of functions including emotion, behavior, motivation, long-term memory, and olfaction. Etymology
	The term 'limbic' comes from the Latin limbus, for 'border' or 'edge'. Anatomy
	The limbic system is the set of brain structures that forms the inner border of the cortex.
Olfactory bulb	The olfactory bulb is a structure of the vertebrate forebrain involved in olfaction, the perception of odors.
	In most vertebrates, the olfactory bulb is the most rostral (forward) part of the brain. In humans, however, the olfactory bulb is on the inferior (bottom) side of the brain.
Lie detection	Lie detection is the practice of determining whether someone is lying. Activities of the body not easily controlled by the conscious mind are compared under different circumstances. Usually this involves asking the subject control questions where the answers are known to the examiner and comparing them to questions where the answers are not known.
Facial expression	A facial expression results from one or more motions or positions of the muscles of the face. These movements convey the emotional state of the individual to observers. Facial expressions are a form of nonverbal communication.
Facial feedback hypothesis	The facial feedback hypothesis states that facial movement can influence emotional experience.

	For example, an individual who is forced to smile during a social event will actually come to find the event more of an enjoyable experience. '
	The free expression by outward signs of an emotion intensifies it.'
Electromyography	Electromyography is a technique for evaluating and recording the electrical activity produced by skeletal muscles. EMG is performed using an instrument called an electromyograph, to produce a record called an electromyogram. An electromyograph detects the electrical potential generated by muscle cells when these cells are electrically or neurologically activated.
Facial electromyography	Facial Electromyography refers to an electromyography (EMG) technique that measures muscle activity by detecting and amplifying the tiny electrical impulses that are generated by muscle fibers when they contract.
	It primarily focuses on two major muscle groups in the face, the corrugator supercilli group which is associated with frowning and the zygomaticus major muscle group which is associated with smiling. Uses
	Facial EMG has been studied to assess its utility as a tool for measuring emotional reaction.
Microexpression	A microexpression is a brief, involuntary facial expression shown on the face of humans according to emotions experienced. They usually occur in high-stakes situations, where people have something to lose or gain. Unlike regular facial expressions, it is difficult to hide microexpression reactions.
Castration	Castration is any action, surgical, chemical, or otherwise, by which a male loses the functions of the testicles or a female loses the functions of the ovaries.
	Humans
	The practice of castration has its roots before recorded human history. Castration was frequently used for religious or social reasons in certain cultures in Europe, the Middle East, South Asia, Africa, East Asia.
Chronic stress	Chronic stress is the response to emotional pressure suffered for a prolonged period over which an individual perceives he or she has no control. It involves an endocrine system response in which occurs a release of corticosteroids. If this continues for a long time, it can cause damage to an individual's physical and mental health.
Convergence	Precisely every individual in the population is identical.

	While full convergence might be seen in genetic algorithms using only cross over, such convergence is seldom seen in genetic programming using Koza's subtree swapping crossover. However, populations often stabilise after a time, in the sense that the best programs all have a common ancestor and their behaviour is very similar both to each other and to that of high fitness programs from the previous generations.
Stressor	A stressor is a chemical or biological agent, environmental condition, external stimulus or an event that causes stress to an organism. An event that triggers the stress response may include:•environmental stressors (elevated sound levels, over-illumination, overcrowding)•daily stress events (e.g. traffic, lost keys)•life changes (e.g. divorce, bereavement)•workplace stressors (e.g. role strain, lack of control)•physical stressors (e.g. tobacco, alcohol, drugs) Stressors have a chemical reaction inside of the body. A harmful stressor is detected by the brain, and a elemental decision pattern occurs.
Adrenal cortex	Situated along the perimeter of the adrenal gland, the adrenal cortex mediates the stress response through the production of mineralocorticoids and glucocorticoids, including aldosterone and cortisol respectively. It is also a secondary site of androgen synthesis.
Adrenal medulla	The adrenal medulla is part of the adrenal gland. It is located at the center of the gland, being surrounded by the adrenal cortex. It is the innermost part of the adrenal gland, consisting of cells that secrete epinephrine, norepinephrine, and a small amount of dopamine in response to stimulation by sympathetic preganglionic neurons.
Adrenocorticotropic hormone	Adrenocorticotropic hormone also known as corticotropin, is a polypeptide tropic hormone produced and secreted by the anterior pituitary gland. It is an important component of the hypothalamic-pituitary-adrenal axis and is often produced in response to biological stress (along with its precursor corticotropin-releasing hormone from the hypothalamus). Its principal effects are increased production and release of corticosteroids.
Dominance hierarchy	A dominance hierarchy is the organization of individuals in a group that occurs when competition for resources leads to aggression. Schjelderup-Ebbe, who studied the often-cited example of the pecking order in chickens, found that such social structures lead to more stable flocks with reduced aggression among individuals. Dominance hierarchies can be despotic or linear.
Epinephrine	Epinephrine is a hormone and a neurotransmitter. Epinephrine has many functions in the body, regulating heart rate, blood vessel and air passage diameters, and metabolic shifts; epinephrine release is a crucial component of the fight-or-flight response of the sympathetic nervous system.

Chapter 17. Biopsychology of Emotion, Stress, and Health

Glucocorticoid	Glucocorticoids (GC) are a class of steroid hormones that bind to the glucocorticoid receptor (GR), which is present in almost every vertebrate animal cell. Glucocorticoids are part of the feedback mechanism in the immune system that turns immune activity (inflammation) down. They are therefore used in medicine to treat diseases that are caused by an overactive immune system, such as allergies, asthma, autoimmune diseases and sepsis. Glucocorticoids have many diverse (pleiotropic) effects, including potentially harmful side effects, and as a result are rarely sold over-the-counter. They also interfere with some of the abnormal mechanisms in cancer cells, so they are used in high doses to treat cancer.
Adrenal glands	In mammals, the adrenal glands are endocrine glands that sit at the top of the kidneys; in humans, the right adrenal gland is triangular shaped, while the left adrenal gland is semilunar shaped. They are chiefly responsible for releasing hormones in response to stress through the synthesis of corticosteroids such as cortisol and catecholamines such as epinephrine (adrenaline) and norepinephrine. They also produce androgens.
Antibody	An antibody is a large Y-shaped protein used by the immune system to identify and neutralize foreign objects like bacteria and viruses. The antibody recognizes a unique part of the foreign target, termed an antigen. Each tip of the 'Y' of an antibody contains a paratope (a structure analogous to a lock) that is specific for one particular epitope (that is equivelent to a key) on an antigen, allowing these two structures to bind together with precision. Using this binding mechanism, an antibody can tag a microbe or an infected cell for attack by other parts of the immune system, or can neutralize its target directly (for example, by blocking a part of a microbe that is essential for its invasion and survival). The production of antibodies is the main function of the humoral immune system.
Cell-mediated immunity	Cell-mediated immunity is an immune response that does not involve antibodies or complement but rather involves the activation of macrophages, natural killer cells (NK), antigen-specific cytotoxic T-lymphocytes, and the release of various cytokines in response to an antigen. Historically, the immune system was separated into two branches: humoral immunity, for which the protective function of immunization could be found in the humor (cell-free bodily fluid or serum) and cellular immunity, for which the protective function of immunization was associated with cells. CD4 cells or helper T cells provide protection against different pathogens.
Macrophage	The terms 'macrophage' and 'microphage' are used in ecology to describe heterotrophs that consume food in two different ways. Both macrophages and microphages 'ingest solid food and may process it through some sort of alimentary canal.' However, a macrophage 'handles food items singly, while a microphage handles food items in bulk without manipulating them individually.' Microphages include suspension feeders, and often incidentally digest low-quality food items.

Psychoneuroimmunology	Psychoneuroimmunology is the study of the interaction between psychological processes and the nervous and immune systems of the human body. PNI takes an interdisciplinary approach, incorporating psychology, neuroscience, immunology, physiology, pharmacology, molecular biology, psychiatry, behavioral medicine, infectious diseases, endocrinology, and rheumatology. The main interests of PNI are the interactions between the nervous and immune systems and the relationships between mental processes and health.
Meta-analysis	In statistics, a meta-analysis combines the results of several studies that address a set of related research hypotheses. In its simplest form, this is normally by identification of a common measure of effect size, for which a weighted average might be the output of a meta-analyses. Here the weighting might be related to sample sizes within the individual studies.
Neuropeptide	Neuropeptides are small protein-like molecules used by neurons to communicate with each other, distinct from the larger neurotransmitters. They are neuronal signaling molecules, influence the activity of the brain in specific ways and are thus involved in particular brain functions, like analgesia, reward, food intake, learning and memory. Neuropeptides are expressed and released by neurons, and mediate or modulate neuronal communication by acting on cell surface receptors.
Spandrel	In evolutionary biology, a Spandrel is a phenotypic characteristic that is a byproduct of the evolution of some other characteristic, rather than a direct product of adaptive selection. The term was coined by the Harvard paleontologist Stephen Jay Gould and population geneticist Richard Lewontin in their influential paper 'The Spandrels of San Marco and the Panglossian Paradigm: A Critique of the Adaptationist Programme' (1979). In this paper Gould and Lewontin employed the analogy of spandrels in Renaissance architecture: curved areas of masonry between arches supporting a dome that arise as a consequence of decisions about the shape of the arches and the base of the dome, rather than being designed for the artistic purposes for which they were often employed.
Granule cell	In neuroscience, granule cells refer to tiny neurons (a type of cell) that are around 10 micrometres in diameter. Granule cells are found within the granular layer of the cerebellum (which is also known as layer 3, the inner most layer of cerebellar cortex with the middle layer being the Purkinje cell layer and the outermost being the Molecular layer), the dentate gyrus of the hippocampus, the superficial layer of the dorsal cochlear nucleus, and in the olfactory bulb.
Prenatal stress	Prenatal stress is exposure of an expectant mother to distress, which can be caused by stressful life events or by environmental hardships.

	The resulting changes to the mother's hormonal and immune system may harm the fetus's (and after birth, the infant's) immune function and brain development. Prenatal stress is shown to have several affects in fetal brain development.
Neurogenesis	Neurogenesis is the process by which neurons are generated from neural stem and progenitor cells. Most active during pre-natal development, neurogenesis is responsible for populating the growing brain with neurons. Recently neurogenesis was shown to continue in several small parts of the brain of mammals: the hippocampus and the subventricular zone.
Estradiol	Estradiol is a sex hormone. Estradiol is the predominant sex hormone present in females. It is also present in males, being produced as an active metabolic product of testosterone. It represents the major estrogen in humans. Estradiol has not only a critical impact on reproductive and sexual functioning, but also affects other organs including the bones.
Fear conditioning	Fear conditioning is a behavioral paradigm in which organisms learn to predict aversive events. It is a form of learning in which an aversive stimulus (e.g. an electrical shock) is associated with a particular neutral context (e.g., a room) or neutral stimulus (e.g., a tone), resulting in the expression of fear responses to the originally neutral stimulus or context. This can be done by pairing the neutral stimulus with an aversive stimulus (e.g., a shock, loud noise, or unpleasant odor).
Periaqueductal gray	Periaqueductal gray is the gray matter located around the cerebral aqueduct within the tegmentum of the midbrain. It plays a role in the descending modulation of pain and in defensive behaviour. The ascending pain and temperature fibers of the spinothalamic tract also send information to the PAG via the spinomesencephalic tract .
Prosody	In linguistics, prosody is the rhythm, stress, and intonation of speech. Prosody may reflect various features of the speaker or the utterance: the emotional state of the speaker; the form of the utterance (statement, question, or command); the presence of irony or sarcasm; emphasis, contrast, and focus; or other elements of language that may not be encoded by grammar or choice of vocabulary. In terms of acoustics, the prosodics of oral languages involve variation in syllable length, loudness and pitch.
Extraversion-introversion	The trait of extraversion-introversion is a central dimension of human personality theories. The terms introversion and extraversion were first popularized by Carl Jung, although both the popular understanding and psychological usage differ from his original intent.

| Neuroticism | Neuroticism is a fundamental personality trait in the study of psychology. It is an enduring tendency to experience negative emotional states. Individuals who score high on neuroticism are more likely than the average to experience such feelings as anxiety, anger, envy, guilt, and depressed mood. |

1. Precisely every individual in the population is identical. While full _____ might be seen in genetic algorithms using only cross over, such _____ is seldom seen in genetic programming using Koza's subtree swapping crossover. However, populations often stabilise after a time, in the sense that the best programs all have a common ancestor and their behaviour is very similar both to each other and to that of high fitness programs from the previous generations.

   a. Cooperative coevolution
   b. Human-based evolutionary computation
   c. HyperNEAT
   d. Convergence

2. The _____ states that facial movement can influence emotional experience. For example, an individual who is forced to smile during a social event will actually come to find the event more of an enjoyable experience. '

   The free expression by outward signs of an emotion intensifies it.'

   a. Facial feedback hypothesis
   b. Multiple Natures
   c. Theory of multiple intelligences
   d. Three Principles

3. _____ is the gray matter located around the cerebral aqueduct within the tegmentum of the midbrain. It plays a role in the descending modulation of pain and in defensive behaviour. The ascending pain and temperature fibers of the spinothalamic tract also send information to the PAG via the spinomesencephalic tract .

   a. Vestibular nuclei
   b. Periaqueductal gray
   c. Functional analytic psychotherapy
   d. Functional contextualism

4. . _____ is the practice of determining whether someone is lying. Activities of the body not easily controlled by the conscious mind are compared under different circumstances. Usually this involves asking the subject control questions where the answers are known to the examiner and comparing them to questions where the answers are not known.

a. Malingering

b. Lie detection

c. Police psychology

d. Psychology, Public Policy and Law

5. _____ is any action, surgical, chemical, or otherwise, by which a male loses the functions of the testicles or a female loses the functions of the ovaries.

Humans

The practice of _____ has its roots before recorded human history. _____ was frequently used for religious or social reasons in certain cultures in Europe, the Middle East, South Asia, Africa, East Asia.

a. Carl Rogers theory evaluation

b. Psychological pain

c. Castration

d. Rational emotive behavior therapy

1. d
2. a
3. b
4. b
5. c

You can take the complete Chapter Practice Test

for Chapter 17. Biopsychology of Emotion, Stress, and Health
on all key terms, persons, places, and concepts.

Online 99 Cents

http://www.epub3.10.9241.17.cram101.com/

Use www.Cram101.com for all your study needs

including Cram101's online interactive problem solving labs in

chemistry, statistics, mathematics, and more.

	Echolalia
	Schizophrenia
	Waxy flexibility
	Chlorpromazine
	Delusion
	Hallucination
	Parkinson's disease
	Butyrophenone
	Haloperidol
	Phenothiazine
	Clozapine
	Affective spectrum
	Depression
	Antidepressant
	Endogenous depression
	Mania
	Fluoxetine
	Imipramine
	Iproniazid

Chapter 18. Biopsychology of Psychiatric Disorders

CHAPTER OUTLINE: KEY TERMS, PEOPLE, PLACES, CONCEPTS

- Monoamine oxidase inhibitor
- Mood stabilizer
- Tricyclic antidepressant
- Tyramine
- Adrenocorticotropic hormone
- Anhedonia
- Anxiety
- Anxiety disorder
- Corticotropin-releasing hormone
- Dexamethasone
- Glucocorticoid
- Hypertension
- Tachycardia
- Agoraphobia
- Anticonvulsant
- Benzodiazepine
- Chlordiazepoxide
- Diazepam
- Generalized anxiety disorder

Hypnotic drugs

Muscle relaxant

Obsessive-compulsive disorder

Panic disorder

Posttraumatic stress disorder

Anxiolytic

Psychoactive drug

Elevated plus maze

Serotonin

Coprolalia

Clinical trial

Placebo

Active placebo

Autonomic nervous system

Optic nerve

Thalamus

Oxytocin

Echolalia	Echolalia is the automatic repetition of vocalizations made by another person. It is closely related to echopraxia, the automatic repetition of movements made by another person. The word 'echolalia' is derived from the Greek ?χ?, meaning 'echo' or 'to repeat', and λαλι? (laliá) meaning 'babbling, meaningless talk' (of onomatopoeic origin, from the verb λαλ?ω (laléo), meaning 'to talk').
Schizophrenia	Schizophrenia is a mental disorder characterized by a disintegration of thought processes and of emotional responsiveness. It most commonly manifests as auditory hallucinations, paranoid or bizarre delusions, or disorganized speech and thinking, and it is accompanied by significant social or occupational dysfunction. The onset of symptoms typically occurs in young adulthood, with a global lifetime prevalence of about 0.3-0.7%.
Waxy flexibility	Waxy flexibility is a psychomotor symptom of catatonic schizophrenia which leads to a decreased response to stimuli and a tendency to remain in an immobile posture. For instance, if one were to move the arm of someone with waxy flexibility, they would keep their arm where one moved it until it was moved again, as if it were made from wax. However it is important to note that although waxy flexibility has historically been linked to schizophrenia, there are also other disorders which it may be associated with, for example, mood disorder with catatonic behaviour.
Chlorpromazine	Chlorpromazine is a typical antipsychotic. First synthesized on December 11, 1950, chlorpromazine was the first drug developed with specific antipsychotic action, and would serve as the prototype for the phenothiazine class of drugs, which later grew to comprise several other agents. The introduction of chlorpromazine into clinical use has been described as the single greatest advance in psychiatric care, dramatically improving the prognosis of patients in psychiatric hospitals worldwide; the availability of antipsychotic drugs curtailed indiscriminate use of electroconvulsive therapy and psychosurgery, and was one of the driving forces behind the deinstitutionalization movement.
Delusion	A delusion is a belief that is either mistaken or not substantiated and is held with very strong feelings or opinions and expressed forcefully. In psychiatry, it is defined to be a belief that is pathological (the result of an illness or illness process) and is held despite evidence to the contrary. As a pathology, it is distinct from a belief based on false or incomplete information, dogma, stupidity, poor memory, illusion, or other effects of perception.
Hallucination	A hallucination, in the broadest sense of the word, is a perception in the absence of a stimulus. In a stricter sense, hallucinations are defined as perceptions in a conscious and awake state in the absence of external stimuli which have qualities of real perception, in that they are vivid, substantial, and located in external objective space.

Chapter 18. Biopsychology of Psychiatric Disorders

Parkinson's disease	Parkinson's disease is a degenerative disorder of the central nervous system. It results from the death of dopamine-containing cells in the substantia nigra, a region of the midbrain; the cause of cell-death is unknown. Early in the course of the disease, the most obvious symptoms are movement-related, including shaking, rigidity, slowness of movement and difficulty with walking and gait. Later, cognitive and behavioural problems may arise, with dementia commonly occurring in the advanced stages of the disease. Other symptoms include sensory, sleep and emotional problems. Parkinson's disease is more common in the elderly with most cases occurring after the age of 50.
Butyrophenone	Butyrophenone is a chemical compound (with a ketone functional group); some of its derivatives (called commonly butyrophenones) are used to treat various psychiatric disorders such as schizophrenia, as well as acting as antiemetics. Butyrophenones are a class of pharmaceutical drugs derived from butyrophenone. Examples include:•Haloperidol, the most widely used classical antipsychotic drug in this class•Droperidol, often used for neuroleptanalgesic anesthesia and sedation in intensive-care treatment•Benperidol, the most potent commonly used antipsychotic (200 times more potent than chlorpromazine)•Triperidol, a highly potent antipsychotic (100 times more potent than chlorpromazine
Haloperidol	Haloperidol is a typical antipsychotic. It is in the butyrophenone class of antipsychotic medications and has pharmacological effects similar to the phenothiazines. Haloperidol is an older antipsychotic used in the treatment of schizophrenia and acute psychotic states and delirium.
Phenothiazine	Phenothiazine is an organic compound that occurs in various antipsychotic and antihistaminic drugs. It has the formula $S(C_6H_4)_2NH$. This yellow tricyclic compound is soluble in acetic acid, benzene, and ether. The compound is related to the thiazine-class of heterocyclic compounds. Derivatives of the parent compound find wide use as drugs.
Clozapine	Clozapine is an atypical antipsychotic medication used in the treatment of schizophrenia, and is also used off-label in the treatment of bipolar disorder. In 2005 three pharmaceutical companies marketed this drug: Novartis Pharmaceuticals (manufacturer), Mylan Laboratories and Ivax Pharmaceuticals (market generic clozapine). The first of the atypical antipsychotics to be developed, it was first introduced in Europe in 1971, but was voluntarily withdrawn by the manufacturer in 1975 after it was shown to cause agranulocytosis, a condition involving a dangerous decrease in the number of white blood cells, that led to death in some patients.

Chapter 18. Biopsychology of Psychiatric Disorders

Affective spectrum	The affective spectrum is a grouping of related psychiatric and medical disorders which may accompany bipolar, unipolar, and schizoaffective disorders at statistically higher rates than would normally be expected. These disorders are identified by a common positive response to the same types of pharmacologic treatments. They also aggregate strongly in families and may therefore share common heritable underlying physiologic anomalies.
Depression	Depression is a state of low mood and aversion to activity that can affect a person's thoughts, behavior, feelings and physical well-being. Depressed people may feel sad, anxious, empty, hopeless, worried, helpless, worthless, guilty, irritable, or restless. They may lose interest in activities that once were pleasurable; experience loss of appetite or overeating, have problems concentrating, remembering details, or making decisions; and may contemplate or attempt suicide.
Antidepressant	Antidepressants, are drugs for the treatment of depression. Despite their name, they are often used to treat other conditions, on- or off-label, for conditions such as anxiety disorders, obsessive compulsive disorder, eating disorders, chronic pain, and some hormone-mediated disorders such as dysmenorrhea, and for snoring, migraines, attention-deficit hyperactivity disorder, (ADHD) substance abuse and occasionally even insomnia. Antidepressants are used either alone or combination with other medications.
Endogenous depression	Endogenous Depression is an atypical sub-class of the Mood Disorder, Clinical Depression (A.K.A. Major Depressive Disorder). Endogenous Depression includes patients with treatment-refractory, unipolar, non-psychotic, Major Depressive Disorder, characterized by a dysregulation of the Endogenous Opioid System and not of the Monoaminergic System. Patients who fall in this sub-class typically respond very well to synthetic opioids which act on the μ-opioid receptors and thought to result in increased serotonin production and norepinephrine reuptake inhibition, including Tramadol, Tapentadol, Buprenorphine, and other similar, synthetic, atypical, opioid analgesics.
Mania	Mania is a state of abnormally elevated or irritable mood, arousal, and/or energy levels. In a sense, it is the opposite of depression. Mania is a criterion for certain psychiatric diagnoses.
Fluoxetine	Fluoxetine is an antidepressant of the selective serotonin reuptake inhibitor (SSRI) class. It is manufactured and marketed by Eli Lilly and Company. In combination with olanzapine it is known as symbyax. Fluoxetine is approved for the treatment of major depression (including pediatric depression), obsessive-compulsive disorder (in both adult and pediatric populations), bulimia nervosa, panic disorder and premenstrual dysphoric disorder.
Imipramine	Imipramine is an antidepressant medication, a tricyclic antidepressant of the dibenzazepine group. Imipramine is mainly used in the treatment of major depression and enuresis (inability to control urination).

Iproniazid	Iproniazid is a hydrazine drug used as an antidepressant. It acts as an irreversible and nonselective monoamine oxidase inhibitor (MAOI). Though it has been widely discontinued in most of the world, it is still used in France.
Monoamine oxidase inhibitor	Monoamine oxidase inhibitors (MAOIs) are a class of antidepressant drugs prescribed for the treatment of depression. They are particularly effective in treating atypical depression. Because of potentially lethal dietary and drug interactions, monoamine oxidase inhibitors have historically been reserved as a last line of treatment, used only when other classes of antidepressant drugs (for example selective serotonin reuptake inhibitors and tricyclic antidepressants) have failed.
Mood stabilizer	A mood stabilizer is a psychiatric medication used to treat mood disorders characterized by intense and sustained mood shifts, typically bipolar disorder. Used to treat bipolar disorder, mood stabilizers suppress swings between mania and depression. Mood-stabilizing drugs are also used in borderline personality disorder and Schizoaffective disorder.
Tricyclic antidepressant	Tricyclic antidepressants (TCAs) are heterocyclic chemical compounds used primarily as antidepressants. heir chemical structure, which contains three rings of atoms. The tetracyclic antidepressants (TeCAs), which contain four rings of atoms, are a closely related group of antidepressant compounds.
Tyramine	Tyramine is a naturally-occurring monoamine compound and trace amine derived from the amino acid tyrosine. Tyramine acts as a catecholamine (dopamine, norepinephrine (noradrenaline), epinephrine (adrenaline)) releasing agent. Notably, however, it is unable to cross the blood-brain-barrier (BBB), resulting in only non-psychoactive peripheral sympathomimetic effects.
Adrenocorticotropic hormone	Adrenocorticotropic hormone also known as corticotropin, is a polypeptide tropic hormone produced and secreted by the anterior pituitary gland. It is an important component of the hypothalamic-pituitary-adrenal axis and is often produced in response to biological stress (along with its precursor corticotropin-releasing hormone from the hypothalamus). Its principal effects are increased production and release of corticosteroids.
Anhedonia	In psychology and psychiatry, anhedonia is defined as the inability to experience pleasure from activities usually found enjoyable, e.g. exercise, hobbies, sexual activities or social interactions.

	While earlier definitions of anhedonia emphasized pleasurable experience, more recent models have highlighted the need to consider different aspects of enjoyable behavior, such as motivation or desire to engage in an activity ('motivational anhedonia'), as compared to the level of enjoyment of the activity itself ('consummatory anhedonia').
	According to William James the term was coined by Théodule-Armand Ribot.
Anxiety	Anxiety is a psychological and physiological state characterized by somatic, emotional, cognitive, and behavioral components. The root meaning of the word anxiety is 'to vex or trouble'; in either the absence or presence of psychological stress, anxiety can create feelings of fear, worry, uneasiness and dread. Anxiety is considered to be a normal reaction to stress.
Anxiety disorder	Anxiety disorder is a blanket term covering several different forms of a type of mental illness of abnormal and pathological fear and anxiety. Conditions now considered anxiety disorders only came under the aegis of psychiatry near the end of the 19th century. Gelder, Mayou & Geddes (2005) explain that anxiety disorders are classified in two groups: continuous symptoms and episodic symptoms.
Corticotropin-releasing hormone	Corticotropin-releasing hormone is a polypeptide hormone and neurotransmitter involved in the stress response. It belongs to corticotropin-releasing factor family.
	Corticotropin-releasing hormone is a 41-amino acid peptide derived from a 191-amino acid preprohormone.
Dexamethasone	Dexamethasone is a potent synthetic member of the glucocorticoid class of steroid drugs. It acts as an anti-inflammatory and immunosuppressant. It is 20 to 30 times more potent than the naturally occurring hormone cortisol and 4 to 5 times more potent than prednisone.
Glucocorticoid	Glucocorticoids (GC) are a class of steroid hormones that bind to the glucocorticoid receptor (GR), which is present in almost every vertebrate animal cell.
	Glucocorticoids are part of the feedback mechanism in the immune system that turns immune activity (inflammation) down. They are therefore used in medicine to treat diseases that are caused by an overactive immune system, such as allergies, asthma, autoimmune diseases and sepsis. Glucocorticoids have many diverse (pleiotropic) effects, including potentially harmful side effects, and as a result are rarely sold over-the-counter. They also interfere with some of the abnormal mechanisms in cancer cells, so they are used in high doses to treat cancer.
Hypertension	Hypertension or high blood pressure, sometimes called arterial hypertension, is a chronic medical condition in which the blood pressure in the arteries is elevated. This requires the heart to work harder than normal to circulate blood through the blood vessels.

Tachycardia	Tachycardia comes from the Greek words tachys (rapid or accelerated) and kardia (of the heart). Tachycardia typically refers to a heart rate that exceeds the normal range for a resting heartrate (heartrate in an inactive or sleeping individual). It can be dangerous depending on the speed and type of rhythm.
Agoraphobia	Agoraphobia is an anxiety disorder characterized by anxiety in situations where it is perceived to be difficult or embarrassing to escape. These situations can include, but are not limited to, wide-open spaces, and uncontrollable social situations such as may be met in shopping malls, airports, and on bridges. Agoraphobia is defined within the DSM-IV TR as a subset of panic disorder, involving the fear of incurring a panic attack in those environments.
Anticonvulsant	The anticonvulsants (also commonly known as antiepileptic drugs) are a diverse group of pharmaceuticals used in the treatment of epileptic seizures. Anticonvulsants are also increasingly being used in the treatment of bipolar disorder, since many seem to act as mood stabilizers, and for the treatment of neuropathic pain. The goal of an anticonvulsant is to suppress the rapid and excessive firing of neurons that start a seizure.
Benzodiazepine	A benzodiazepine is a psychoactive drug whose core chemical structure is the fusion of a benzene ring and a diazepine ring. The first benzodiazepine, chlordiazepoxide (Librium), was discovered accidentally by Leo Sternbach in 1955, and made available in 1960 by Hoffmann-La Roche, which has also marketed diazepam (Valium) since 1963. Benzodiazepines enhance the effect of the neurotransmitter gamma-aminobutyric acid (GABA), which results in sedative, hypnotic (sleep-inducing), anxiolytic (anti-anxiety), anticonvulsant, muscle relaxant and amnesic action.
Chlordiazepoxide	Chlordiazepoxide is a sedativehypnotic drug and benzodiazepine. It is marketed under the trade names Angirex, Elenium, Klopoxid, Librax (also contains clidinium bromide), Libritabs, Librium, Mesural, Multum, Novapam, Risolid, Silibrin, Sonimen and Tropium. Chlordiazepoxide was the first benzodiazepine to be synthesised and the discovery of chlordiazepoxide was by pure chance.
Diazepam	Diazepam first marketed as Valium by Hoffmann-La Roche, is a benzodiazepine drug. Diazepam is also marketed in Australia as Antenex. It is commonly used for treating anxiety, insomnia, seizures including status epilepticus, muscle spasms (such as in cases of tetanus), restless legs syndrome, alcohol withdrawal, benzodiazepine withdrawal and Ménière's disease.
Generalized anxiety disorder	Generalized anxiety disorder is an anxiety disorder that is characterized by excessive, uncontrollable and often irrational worry about everyday things that is disproportionate to the actual source of worry.

This excessive worry often interferes with daily functioning, as individuals suffering GAD typically anticipate disaster, and are overly concerned about everyday matters such as health issues, money, death, family problems, friend problems, relationship problems or work difficulties. Individuals often exhibit a variety of physical symptoms, including fatigue, fidgeting, headaches, nausea, numbness in hands and feet, muscle tension, muscle aches, difficulty swallowing, bouts of difficulty breathing, difficulty concentrating, trembling, twitching, irritability, agitation, sweating, restlessness, insomnia, hot flashes, and rashes and inability to fully control the anxiety (ICD-10).

Hypnotic drugs

Hypnotic drugs are a class of psychoactives whose primary function is to induce sleep and to be used in the treatment of insomnia and in surgical anesthesia. When used in anesthesia to produce and maintain unconsciousness, 'sleep' is metaphorical and there are no regular sleep stages or cyclical natural states; patients rarely recover from anesthesia feeling refreshed and with renewed energy. Because drugs in this class generally produce dose-dependent effects, ranging from anxiolysis to production of unconsciousness, they are often referred to collectively as sedative-hypnotic drugs.

Muscle relaxant

A muscle relaxant is a drug which affects skeletal muscle function and decreases the muscle tone. It may be used to alleviate symptoms such as muscle spasms, pain, and hyperreflexia. The term 'muscle relaxant' is used to refer to two major therapeutic groups: neuromuscular blockers and spasmolytics. Neuromuscular blockers act by interfering with transmission at the neuromuscular end plate and have no CNS activity. They are often used during surgical procedures and in intensive care and emergency medicine to cause paralysis. Spasmolytics, also known as 'centrally-acting' muscle relaxants, are used to alleviate musculoskeletal pain and spasms and to reduce spasticity in a variety of neurological conditions. While both neuromuscular blockers and spasmolytics are often grouped together as muscle relaxants, the term is commonly used to refer to spasmolytics only.

Obsessive-compulsive disorder

Obsessive-compulsive disorder is an anxiety disorder characterized by intrusive thoughts that produce uneasiness, apprehension, fear, or worry, by repetitive behaviors aimed at reducing anxiety, or by a combination of such thoughts (obsessions) and behaviors (compulsions). Symptoms may include repetitive handwashing; extensive hoarding; preoccupation with sexual or aggressive impulses, or with particular religious beliefs; aversion to odd numbers; and nervous habits, such as opening a door and closing it a certain number of times before one enters or leaves a room. These symptoms can be alienating and time-consuming, and often cause severe emotional and financial distress.

Panic disorder

Panic disorder is an anxiety disorder characterized by recurring severe panic attacks. It may also include significant behavioral changes lasting at least a month and of ongoing worry about the implications or concern about having other attacks.

Posttraumatic stress disorder	Posttraumatic stress disorder is a severe anxiety disorder that can develop after exposure to any event that results in psychological trauma. This event may involve the threat of death to oneself or to someone else, or to one's own or someone else's physical, sexual, or psychological integrity, overwhelming the individual's ability to cope. As an effect of psychological trauma, PTSD is less frequent and more enduring than the more commonly seen acute stress response.
Anxiolytic	An anxiolytic is a drug used for the treatment of anxiety and its related psychological and physical symptoms. Anxiolytics have been shown to be useful in the treatment of anxiety disorders. Beta-receptor blockers such as propranolol and oxprenolol, although not anxiolytics, can be used to combat the somatic symptoms of anxiety.
Psychoactive drug	A psychoactive drug, psychopharmaceutical, or psychotropic is a chemical substance that crosses the blood-brain barrier and acts primarily upon the central nervous system where it affects brain function, resulting in changes in perception, mood, consciousness, cognition, and behavior. These substances may be used recreationally, to purposefully alter one's consciousness, as entheogens, for ritual, spiritual, and/or shamanic purposes, as a tool for studying or augmenting the mind, or therapeutically as medication. Because psychoactive substances bring about subjective changes in consciousness and mood that the user may find pleasant (e.g. euphoria) or advantageous (e.g. increased alertness), many psychoactive substances are abused, that is, used excessively, despite the health risks or negative consequences.
Elevated plus maze	The elevated plus maze is a rodent model of anxiety that is used as a screening test for putative anxiolytic or anxiogenic compounds and as a general research tool in neurobiological anxiety research. The test setting consists of a plus-shaped apparatus with two open and two enclosed arms, each with an open roof, elevated 40-70 cm from the floor. The model is based on rodents' aversion of open spaces.
Serotonin	Serotonin is a monoamine neurotransmitter. Biochemically derived from tryptophan, serotonin is primarily found in the gastrointestinal (GI) tract, platelets, and in the central nervous system (CNS) of animals including humans. It is a well-known contributor to feelings of well-being; therefore it is also known as a 'happiness hormone' despite not being a hormone.
Coprolalia	Coprolalia is involuntary swearing or the involuntary utterance of obscene words or socially inappropriate and derogatory remarks. Coprolalia comes from the Greek κ?προς (kopros) meaning 'feces' and λαλι? (lalia) from lalein, 'to talk'.

Chapter 18. Biopsychology of Psychiatric Disorders

Clinical trial	Clinical trials are a step in medical research conducted to allow safety (or more specifically, information about adverse drug reactions and adverse effects of other treatments) and efficacy data to be collected for health interventions (e.g., drugs, diagnostics, devices, therapy protocols). These trials can take place only after satisfactory information has been gathered on the quality of the non-clinical safety, and Health Authority/Ethics Committee approval is granted in the country where the trial is taking place. Depending on the type of product and the stage of its development, investigators enroll healthy volunteers and/or patients into small pilot studies initially, followed by larger scale studies in patients that often compare the new product with the currently prescribed treatment.
Placebo	A placebo is a simulated or otherwise medically ineffectual treatment for a disease or other medical condition intended to deceive the recipient. Sometimes patients given a placebo treatment will have a perceived or actual improvement in a medical condition, a phenomenon commonly called the placebo effect. In medical research, placebos are given as control treatments and depend on the use of measured deception.
Active placebo	An active placebo is a placebo that mimics the common side effects of the drug under study. According to a 1965 paper, the term 'fake placebo' was suggested in a 1959 paper published in German. Example Morphine and gabapentin are painkillers with the common side effects of sleepiness and dizziness.
Autonomic nervous system	The autonomic nervous system is the part of the peripheral nervous system that acts as a control system functioning largely below the level of consciousness, and controls visceral functions. The Autonomic nervous system affects heart rate, digestion, respiration rate, salivation, perspiration, diameter of the pupils, micturition (urination), and sexual arousal. Whereas most of its actions are involuntary, some, such as breathing, work in tandem with the conscious mind.
Optic nerve	The optic nerve, transmits visual information from the retina to the brain. Derived from the embryonic retinal ganglion cell, a diverticulum located in the diencephalon, the optic nerve does not regenerate after transection.

Thalamus	The thalamus is a midline symmetrical structure within the brains of vertebrates including humans, situated between the cerebral cortex and midbrain. Its function includes relaying sensory and motor signals to the cerebral cortex, along with the regulation of consciousness, sleep, and alertness. The thalamus surrounds the third ventricle.
Oxytocin	Oxytocin ( ) is a mammalian hormone that acts primarily as a neuromodulator in the brain. Oxytocin is best known for its roles in sexual reproduction, in particular during and after childbirth. It is released in large amounts after distension of the cervix and uterus during labor, facilitating birth, and after stimulation of the nipples, facilitating breastfeeding.

1. _____ is a naturally-occurring monoamine compound and trace amine derived from the amino acid tyrosine. _____ acts as a catecholamine (dopamine, norepinephrine (noradrenaline), epinephrine (adrenaline)) releasing agent. Notably, however, it is unable to cross the blood-brain-barrier (BBB), resulting in only non-psychoactive peripheral sympathomimetic effects.

   a. Varacin
   b. Carl Rogers theory evaluation
   c. massed learning
   d. Tyramine

2. _____ is a mental disorder characterized by a disintegration of thought processes and of emotional responsiveness. It most commonly manifests as auditory hallucinations, paranoid or bizarre delusions, or disorganized speech and thinking, and it is accompanied by significant social or occupational dysfunction. The onset of symptoms typically occurs in young adulthood, with a global lifetime prevalence of about 0.3-0.7%.

   a. Brief psychotic disorder
   b. Clinical lycanthropy
   c. Cotard delusion
   d. Schizophrenia

3. . _____ are a class of psychoactives whose primary function is to induce sleep and to be used in the treatment of insomnia and in surgical anesthesia. When used in anesthesia to produce and maintain unconsciousness, 'sleep' is metaphorical and there are no regular sleep stages or cyclical natural states; patients rarely recover from anesthesia feeling refreshed and with renewed energy. Because drugs in this class generally produce dose-dependent effects, ranging from anxiolysis to production of unconsciousness, they are often referred to collectively as sedative-
   _____ .

a. massed learning
b. Hypersexuality
c. Hypoactive sexual desire disorder
d. Hypnotic drugs

4. _____ is an organic compound that occurs in various antipsychotic and antihistaminic drugs. It has the formula S$(C_6H_4)_2$NH. This yellow tricyclic compound is soluble in acetic acid, benzene, and ether. The compound is related to the thiazine-class of heterocyclic compounds. Derivatives of the parent compound find wide use as drugs.

a. Carl Rogers theory evaluation
b. Phenothiazine
c. Lorazepam
d. Metopimazine

5. A _____ is a belief that is either mistaken or not substantiated and is held with very strong feelings or opinions and expressed forcefully. In psychiatry, it is defined to be a belief that is pathological (the result of an illness or illness process) and is held despite evidence to the contrary. As a pathology, it is distinct from a belief based on false or incomplete information, dogma, stupidity, poor memory, illusion, or other effects of perception.

a. Delusion
b. Collective belief
c. Consensus reality
d. Doctrine

1. d
2. d
3. d
4. b
5. a

You can take the complete Chapter Practice Test

for Chapter 18. Biopsychology of Psychiatric Disorders
on all key terms, persons, places, and concepts.

Online 99 Cents

http://www.epub3.10.9241.18.cram101.com/

Use www.Cram101.com for all your study needs

including Cram101's online interactive problem solving labs in

chemistry, statistics, mathematics, and more.

Other Cram101 e-Books and Tests

Want More?
Cram101.com...

Cram101.com provides the outlines and highlights of your textbooks, just like this e-StudyGuide, but also gives you the PRACTICE TESTS, and other exclusive study tools for all of your textbooks.

Learn More. *Just click*
http://www.cram101.com/

Other Cram101 e-Books and Tests

Lightning Source UK Ltd.
Milton Keynes UK
UKHW051914031120
372738UK00009B/116